RHAPSODY FOR THE THEATRE

RHAPSODY FOR THE THEATRE

ALAIN BADIOU

Edited and Introduced
by Bruno Bosteels

Translated by Bruno Bosteels
with the Assistance of
Martin Puchner

VERSO
London • New York

This English-language edition published by Verso 2013

Chapter 1 first published as *Rhapsodie pour le théâtre: Court traité philosophique*

Chapter 2 first published as *Théâtre et philosophie*

Chapter 3 first published as 'Destin politique du théâtre, hier, maintenant', the preface to *Au temps de l'anarchie, un théâtre de combat, 1880–1914*, Jonny Ebstein, Philippe Ivernel, Monique Surel-Tupin, and Sylvie Thomas, eds

Chapter 4 first published as 'Notes sur *Les Séquestrés d'Altona*' in *Revue internationale de philosophie* 2005
Chapter 5 first published as the preface to Alain Badiou's *La Tétralogie d'Ahmed*

1 3 5 7 9 10 8 6 4 2

Verso
UK: 6 Meard Street, London W1F 0EG
US: 20 Jay Street, Suite 1010, Brooklyn, NY 11201
www.versobooks.com

Verso is the imprint of New Left Books

ISBN-13: 978-1-78168-125-1 (pbk)
ISBN-13: 978-1-78168-126-8 (hbk)

British Library Cataloguing in Publication Data
A catalogue record for this book is available from the British Library

Library of Congress Cataloging-in-Publication Data
A catalog record for this book is available from the Library of Congress

Typeset in Sabon by MJ & N Gavan, Truro, Cornwall
Printed in the US by Maple Vail

CONTENTS

INTRODUCTION

This volume, following closely on the heels of *The Adventure of French Philosophy*, gathers most of Alain Badiou's writings on theatre, including – in the last two texts – reflections on his own art as a playwright and its relation to his work as a philosopher. The core of the volume is made up of the translation of *Rhapsodie pour le théâtre: Court traité philosophique* ('Rhapsody for the Theatre: A Short Philosophical Treatise'), much of which was first published in French between 1986 and 1989 as a series of short interventions in the journal *L'Art du Théâtre*, linked to the project of the important theatre director and Badiou's long-time collaborator, Antoine Vitez; and then, in 1990, in the form of a book.[1]

1. Alain Badiou, *Rhapsodie pour le théâtre: Court traité philosophique* (Paris: L'Imprimerie Nationale, 1990). Prior to this treatise, Badiou had discussed Greek tragedy by contrasting the dominant Sophoclean model with the Aeschylean one, in 'Lack and Destruction', in *Theory of the Subject*, trans. Bruno Bosteels (London: Continuum, 2009), pp. 111–76. Most recently, see also Alain Badiou with Nicolas Truong, *Éloge du théâtre* (Paris: Flammarion, 2013). Badiou's relation to the theatre in general is studied in Oliver Feltham, 'An Explosive

'Rhapsody for the Theatre' occupies a unique spot in Badiou's oeuvre. Part philosophy and part theatre, or at least proto-theatre, it certainly can be read alongside other books from the same period, especially *Handbook of Inaesthetics* and *Metapolitics*, devoted respectively to the truth procedures of art and politics that function as two of the four conditions of philosophy according to Badiou.[2] Of the other two conditions, mathematics is treated in *Number and Numbers* and *Briefings on Existence: A Short Treatise on Transitory Ontology*, whereas for a long time, that is, until the recent publication of the dialogue *In Praise of Love*, love was the only truth procedure not to have received a book-length investigation.[3] Yet, even in the case of Badiou's early treatment of love, a text such as 'The Scene of the Two' resonates with the discussion of theatre due to the importance given to the production of a 'scene'

Genealogy: Theatre, Philosophy and the Art of Presentation', in *The Praxis of Alain Badiou*, ed. Paul Ashton, A.J. Bartlett and Justin Clemens (Melbourne: re.press, 2006), pp. 247–64; Martin Puchner, 'The Theatre of Alain Badiou', *Theatre Research International* 34.3 (2009), pp. 256–66; and Kenneth Reinhard, 'Badiou's Theater: A Laboratory for Thinking,' in Alain Badiou, *The Incident at Antioch: A Tragedy in Three Acts*, trans. Susan Spitzer (New York: Columbia University Press, 2013), xxi–li. Badiou also discusses the current state of theatre in relation to the impact of happenings and performances, in 'A Theatre of Operations: A Discussion between Alain Badiou and Elie During', in *A Theater without Theater* (Barcelona: Museu d'Art Contemporani de Barcelona, 2008), pp. 22–7. For a comparison with Rancière and Virno, see Simon Bayly, 'Theatre and the Public: Badiou, Rancière, Virno', *Radical Philosophy* 157 (2009), pp. 20–9.

2. Alain Badiou, *Handbook of Inaesthetics*, trans. Alberto Toscano (Stanford: Stanford University Press, 2005); *Metapolitics*, trans. Jason Barker (London: Verso, 2005). Earlier, Badiou also discusses politics in *Peut-on penser la politique?* (Paris: Seuil, 1985).

3. Alain Badiou, *Number and Numbers* (Cambridge: Polity Press, 2008); *Briefings on Existence: A Short Treatise on Transitory Ontology*, trans. Norman Madarasz (Albany: SUNY Press, 2006); and *In Praise of Love*, trans. Peter Bush (London: Serpent's Tail, 2012).

or 'stage' (in French, *scène* can designate both) for the amorous couple, just as Freudian psychoanalysis studied how dreams could produce 'another scene', *eine andere Schauplatz*, for the fulfillment of desire and the staging of fantasy. 'I will thus posit that love is precisely this: the advent of the Two as such, the scene of Two,' writes Badiou. 'Love is that scene in which a truth proceeds, a truth about the sexuated positions through a conflict of knowledges for which there can be no compensation.'[4] The scene of love, however, does not present the being of sexual difference as a static given; it requires work, an ongoing process and a series of operations for allowing difference and disjunction to appear in the form of a couple. Badiou's treatments of love and politics thus converge with many of his presuppositions regarding the art of the stage: 'When all is said and done, theater thinks, in the space opened between life and death, the knot that binds together desire and politics. It thinks this knot in the form of an event, that is, in the form of the intrigue or the catastrophe.'[5]

---

4. Alain Badiou, 'What Is Love?' in *Conditions*, trans. Steven Corcoran (London: Continuum, 2008), pp. 188 and 195. See also Alain Badiou, 'The Scene of Two', trans. Barbara P. Fulks, *Lacanian Ink* 21 (2003), pp. 42–55. With regard to the use of theatrical references in psychoanalysis, Louis Althusser also writes: 'From Politzer, who talks of "drama" to Freud and Lacan who speak of theatre, stage, *mise en scène*, machinery, theatrical genre, *metteur en scène*, etc., there is all the distance between the spectator who takes himself for the theatre – and the theatre itself,' in Louis Althusser, 'Freud and Lacan', in *Lenin and Philosophy and Other Essays*, trans. Ben Brewster (New York: Monthly Review Press, 1971), p. 216 n. 7. I owe this reference to Andrew Bielski, from Cornell University, who currently is doing fascinating work on the relationship between theatre and psychoanalysis. For a sharp critique of Badiou's views on theatre and sexuation, see Muriel Plana, 'Le désir masculin du féminin: la théorie d'Alain Badiou', in *Théâtre et féminin: identité, sexualité, politique* (Dijon: Éditions Universitaires de Dijon, 2012), pp. 263–7.

5. Badiou, 'Theses on Theater', in *Handbook of Inaesthetics*, p. 73.

In addition to opening up a fascinating dialogue with the theoretical treatment of the four conditions of philosophy for Badiou, 'Rhapsody for the Theatre' also and at the same time can serve as an accompanying piece for Badiou's work as a playwright – beginning with the 'novel-opera' from the Maoist years, *L'Écharpe rouge*, and culminating in the Ahmed cycle or tetralogy that is made up of *Ahmed le subtil, Ahmed philosophe, Ahmed se fâche,* and *Les Citrouilles* and that was put on stage in a quick creative sequence starting just four years after the publication of 'Rhapsody for the Theatre'.[6] In fact,

6. Alain Badiou, *L'Écharpe rouge: romanopéra* (Paris: François Maspero, 1979); *Ahmed le subtil: Farce en trois actes* (Arles: Actes Sud, 1994); *Ahmed philosophe: Vingt-deux petites pièces pour les enfants et pour les autres,* suivi de *Ahmed se fâche: Comédie en quatre mouvements* (Arles: Actes Sud, 1997); *Les Citrouilles* (Arles: Actes Sud, 1996). More recently, all four Ahmed plays have also been collected into a single volume, *La Tétralogie d'Ahmed: Ahmed le subtil, Ahmed philosophe, Ahmed se fâche, Les Citrouilles* (Arles: Actes Sud, 2009). For a detailed analysis of *L'Écharpe rouge*, see Emily Apter, 'Laws of the '70s: Badiou's Revolutionary Untimeliness', *Cardozo Law Review* 29.5 (April 2008), pp. 1885–1904. Badiou's first play was also already discussed in the newsletter of the Maoist Groupe Foudre, which was the arm of cultural and artistic intervention of the Union des Communistes de France Marxiste-Léniniste (UCFML) in which Badiou was a militant throughout the 1970s. See the article signed by 'L.S.', '*L'Écharpe rouge* ou la question d'un "art marxiste" ', *Feuille Foudre: Revue du Groupe Foudre* 6 (1980), pp. 25–30. Badiou's adaptation of Molière's *Les Fourberies de Scapin* in *Ahmed le subtil* is the topic of the early article by Jean-Yves Coquelin, 'La traversée du masque: Sur *Ahmed le subtil*', *Théâtre/Public* 129 (May 1996), pp. 59–63. In the same journal, as part of a special issue on 'La "geste" d'Ahmed', see also the interview with Chantal Boiron, 'Un opératoire théâtral', *Théâtre/Public* 129 (May 1996), pp. 52–8. For a comparative analysis of *L'Écharpe rouge* and *Ahmed le subtil*, particularly in relation to Badiou's changing views of emancipatory politics as taking place at a distance from the State, see Olivier Neveux, 'La déclaration d'État: Sur le "théâtre politique" d'Alain Badiou', *Actuel Marx* 38 (2005), pp. 179–92. See also Janelle Reinelt, 'Theatre and Politics: Encountering Badiou', *Performance Research* 9.4 (2004), pp. 87–94. Finally, while *Ahmed philosophe* is forthcoming in English in a translation by Joe Litvak, Susan Spitzer's recent translation

one of the most intriguing aspects of this treatise is the way in which it too already moves between philosophy and theatre to the point of opening up a space of indiscernibility between the two.

With the intermittent and hilarious dialogue between 'the Empiricist' and 'Me' in 'Rhapsody for the Theatre', for instance, we seem to be on the verge of becoming privy to the rehearsals for an actual theatre event, whose essence it is the treatise's aim to define and defend against its rivaling forms, if not its simulacra, that would be 'theatre', cinema, and the religious mass. It is almost as though, by some strange inner force, the philosophical reflection on theatre in turn develops its own theatrical potential and, in a process of tempting fits and starts, is about to become a play in its own right. No great leap of the imagination or change in style would be required, for example, to allow portions of 'Rhapsody for the Theatre' to pass over into something along the lines of *Les Citrouilles*, a rewriting of Aristophanes' comedy *The Frogs* and the last of the Ahmed plays in which Badiou has his main character descend into Theatre Hell and argue it out with an unforgiving Chorus over who is the greater playwright of the twentieth century, Bertold Brecht or Paul Claudel, in terms of what each of them might contribute to an overcoming of the 'crisis' of theatre today.

Much of Badiou's conceptual proposition in 'Rhapsody for the Theatre' centres on a bold analogy between theatre and politics. In fact, after having started his career as a most promising novelist, author of the

---

of *The Incident at Antioch* also includes the previously unpublished French version, *L'Incident d'Antioche*. See Alain Badiou, *Ahmed the Philosopher*, trans. Joe Litvak (New York: Columbia University Press, 2013); and *The Incident at Antioch: a Tragedy in Three Acts/L'Incident d'Antioche: Tragédie en trois actes*, trans. Susan Spitzer, with an introduction by Kenneth Reinhard (New York: Columbia University Press, 2013).

novels or anti-novels *Almagestes* and *Portulans*, who drew much praise at the time from Jean-Paul Sartre, a growing awareness of the eminently political destiny of theatre pulled Badiou away from the form of the novel and back to his childhood love for the art of the stage. 'Under the conditions of the time, heavily marked by militantism and commitment, there was something in the writing of novels that seemed too slow to me, and by contrast I became convinced that in the theatre it was possible to engage with the debate on the spot and immediately', explains Badiou. 'I was convinced that theatre was the most appropriate form of artistic expression for everything pertaining to conflict, through the figure of the dialogue, and to opposition.'[7]

Badiou specifically sees the connection to politics as being mediated in turn through the privileged relation of theatre to the State. In his major philosophical book, *Being and Event*, Badiou defines the latter by playing on both the strictly political meaning of the term (the State) and its everyday usage (a state of affairs). What enables this play is a common representational operation, that is, ways of re-presenting or counting a second time that which already is taken to define what counts in the original situation or presentation of things. 'On this point, concrete analysis converges with the philosophical theme: all situations are structured twice. This also means: there is always both presentation and representation', postulates Badiou. 'I will hereinafter term *state of the situation* that by means of which the structure of a situation – of any structured presentation whatsoever – is counted as one, which is to say the one of the one-effect itself.'[8] Theatre's fundamental

7. Badiou, 'Un opérateur théâtral', p. 52.

8. Alain Badiou, 'Meditation Eight: The State, or Metastructure, and the Typology of Being (normality, singularity, excrescence)', in *Being and Event*, trans. Oliver Feltham (London: Continuum, 2005), pp. 94–5.

political significance, according to an argument that Badiou develops throughout 'Rhapsody for the Theatre', consists in adding a further twist to this dialectic of presentation and representation, of situation and state of the situation. Thus, whereas for Badiou – at least after his Maoist years – all emancipatory politics already places the State at a distance by rendering visible and putting some measure on its intrinsically excessive force, theatre introduces an additional figurative distance into this operation by way of a passage through the fiction of a past without which no play seems able to relate to its own present. Theatre not only renders visible the State; it does so by presenting that which cannot but remain invisible and unrepresentable in the existing state of affairs.

Badiou further develops the analogy between theatre and politics to suggest a strict isomorphism between the combinatory of elements that would be constitutive of each of the two. The ensemble of the 'parts of theatre' (and, by extension, the 'parts of politics') becomes activated only in the event of an actual theatre performance (or a militant political intervention), which, as it were, passes through and sublates the 'analytic' of constitutive elements (place, text, director, actors, decor, costumes, and public) into the concepts of a 'dialectic' (involving a spectator-subject, an ethics of play, and a double distancing from the State). This move from the analytic to the dialectic corresponds to the passage from a theatre text to the event of its performance. (In French, Badiou systematically refers to this performative aspect as *représentation*, which I have chosen to translate literally as 'representation', in part because there is no intended dialogue with the field of performance studies in the English-speaking world and in part so as to retain the play on presentation and representation.) No new elements are added in this process but everything is renamed and lifted to a higher level of intensity if and when a theatre event actually takes place.

In addition to the analogy between theatre and politics, elaborated by way of the interplay between the analytical and the dialectical views, Badiou structures much of 'Rhapsody for the Theatre' around a number of other conceptual pairs. The most significant of these are as follows: true theatre (or Theatre) and the simulacrum of 'theatre'; theatre and cinema; theatre and the religious mass; actors and actresses, including a sexuated inquiry into the formulas of imitation without a substance; text and event, or what happens exactly in the move from the analytic to the dialectic; desire and the idea, or theatre as the psychoanalyst's accomplice and as the philosopher's rival; comedy and tragedy, with specific reference to their modern impossibility; and time and eternity, including the idea that theatre produces as it were a history of eternity of its own.

As Badiou himself hints at, the most significant predecessor for a treatise such as 'Rhapsody for the Theatre' without a doubt is Stéphane Mallarmé.[9] Indeed, the

9. See in particular Stéphane Mallarmé, *Igitur*, ed. Robert Greer Cohn (Berkeley: University of California Press, 1981) and *Divagations*, trans. Barbara Johnson (Cambridge: Harvard University Press, 2007). Already in the introductory study for his edition of Mallarmé's manuscript for the Book (*Le Livre*), Jacques Scherer devotes one chapter each to the 'Metaphysics of the Theatre' and to the 'Physics of the Theatre'. See Jacques Scherer, *Le 'Livre' de Mallarmé* (Paris: Gallimard, 1957), pp. 25–45 and 62–74. Incidentally, even the order of these chapters provides us with an interesting anticipation of the way in which Badiou has the 'Metaphysics' of the subject come before the 'Physics' of the subject, in the follow-up to *Being and Event* that is *Logics of Worlds*: 'As you can see, what is "difficult" is not the subject, but the body. Physics is always more difficult than meta-physics,' which is why the 'Formal Theory of the Subject (Meta-physics)' in Book I can come before the answer to the question 'What is a Body?' in Book VII. See Alain Badiou, *Logics of Worlds*, trans. Alberto Toscano (London: Continuum, 2009), p. 50.

latter's influence is both overwhelming and detailed, from the opening mention of the chandelier or lustre as part of theatre's indispensable makeup all the way to the central reflections on the church's conflicted relation to the theatre world, to acting, and to visual pomp of all kinds, when contrasted with its own spectacle of the liturgical mass. Mallarmé's annotations in *Igitur* or in *Divagations*, including 'Scribbled at the Theatre' but also texts such as 'Catholicism', are in fact constantly echoed throughout Badiou's text, creating a subtle system of resonances that still awaits its interpreter. Or, to put this the other way around, nobody interested in the complex relation between Badiou and Mallarmé can afford to ignore 'Rhapsody for the Theatre'.[10]

As to its form, 'Rhapsody for the Theatre' presents itself as a series of what Badiou calls 'paragraphs' but perhaps it is useful to think of them as 'theses'. More so than Karl Marx's paradigmatic 'Theses on Feuerbach' or Walter Benjamin's 'Theses on the Philosophy of History', the closest relative that comes to mind in the French tradition is Guy Debord with *The Society of the Spectacle*.[11] Like Debord, Badiou also delights in

---

10. Puchner begins to spell out the importance of this relation to Mallarmé's dramatism, but he limits his discussion to *Handbook of Inaesthetics* and *Being and Event*. 'Situation, event, throw of dice – the terms of Badiou's discussion of Mallarmé have one thing in common: they are at home in the theatre,' this theatre critic writes. 'Even though Badiou, following Heidegger, discusses Mallarmé under the general rubric of the poem, the more important category is in fact drama.' See Puchner, 'The Theatre of Alain Badiou', p. 262. An overview of Badiou's lifelong critical engagement with Mallarmé would have to include the long chapter 'The Subject under the Signifiers of the Exception', in *Theory of the Subject*, pp. 51–110; 'Mallarmé's Method: Subtraction and Isolation', in *Conditions*, pp. 49–67; Meditation 19 in *Being and Event*; 'A Poetic Dialectic: Labîd ben Rabi'a and Mallarmé' and 'Philosophy of the Faun', both in *Handbook of Inaesthetics*, pp. 46–56 and 122–141; and 'First Provisional Theses on Logic', in *Briefings on Existence*, pp. 119–124.

11. Guy Debord, *The Society of the Spectacle*, trans. Donald

'diverting' (*détourner*) well-known passages, concepts, or characters both historical and fictive, without always indicating as much with quotation marks or an explicit reference. Going partly against this preference on the author's part, a few explanatory footnotes have been added whenever this seemed appropriate and useful. Badiou's own 'Notes, References, Regrets', by contrast, are kept separate at the end of my translation of 'Rhapsody for the Theatre', with numbers referring to the relevant paragraph or thesis in the main text.

'Rhapsody for the Theatre' is followed by a short text, 'Theatre and Philosophy', originally presented as a talk in the context of a conference cycle organized by the Comédie of Reims. Here Badiou develops a thesis that he would take up in greater detail in *Handbook of Inaesthetics*, according to which the relation of philosophy to theatre has adopted the same three forms or figures as the relation of philosophy to art in general. These are the didactic, classical, and romantic figures. For Badiou, twentieth-century theatre has exhaustively tested and ultimately saturated the potential of these three figures, without any genuine innovation. The real difficulty lies rather in inventing a fourth figure, which

Nicholson-Smith (New York: Zone Books, 1994). Louis Althusser, who was Badiou's mentor and in many ways Debord's nemesis, also defines the thesis as the characteristic form taken by the philosopher's theoretical practice: 'Philosophical propositions are Theses'. See Louis Althusser, *Philosophy and the Spontaneous Philosophy of Scientists*, ed. with an introduction by Gregory Elliott (London: Verso, 1990), p. 74. On a related note, Badiou's comments on melodrama and the legacy of Brechtian didacticism, both in 'The Political Destiny of Theatre Yesterday and Today' and in 'The Ahmed Tetralogy', as well as his analysis of Sartre's play *The Condemned of Altona* could be usefully compared to Althusser's detailed analysis of the Piccolo Teatro, in Louis Althusser, 'The "Piccolo Teatro": Bertolazzi and Brecht. Notes on a Materialist Theatre', in *For Marx*, trans. Ben Brewster (London: Verso, 1969), pp. 129–51.

he proposes to call 'immanentist'.[12] This would entail a view in which art is capable of producing a truth that is not external but immanent to the work of art itself. Theatre, too, would thus be capable of producing truths, which Badiou calls 'theatre-ideas' or 'theatre-truths', without having to reduce these to forms of knowledge – not to mention the power of opinions – that would be readily available to the philosopher or the spectator outside the theatre hall. 'To establish – as we must for every art – that theater thinks': such would be the task for the philosopher who wishes to capture the essence of the theatrical event as capable of producing ideas. 'These ideas – and this point is crucial – are *theater-ideas*,' Badiou explains. 'This means they cannot be produced in any other place or by any other means. It also means that none of the components taken separately is capable of producing theater-ideas, not even the text. The idea arises in and by the performance, through the act of theatrical representation.'[13]

Because of the close analogy between theatre and politics, moreover, all theatre-truths also capture some aspect of the popular intelligence of situations and the subjective capacity for emancipatory interventions. This brings Badiou, in 'The Political Destiny of Theatre Yesterday and Today', to revisit the legacy of the socialist and anarchist theatre of the turn of the century, between 1880 and 1914. Though nowadays almost entirely forgotten, if not actively censored and excised from the history books and theatre annals together with the experience of the Paris Commune, this 'combat theatre' serves as a model for the way in which Badiou himself envisions the task and the difficulties that he is up against

12. For Badiou's discussion of the four ways in which philosophy seizes upon art in general, see 'Art and Philosophy', in *Handbook of Inaesthetics*, pp. 1–15.

13. Badiou, 'Theses on Theater', p. 72.

as a playwright who proposes to follow the twentieth-century examples not only of Claudel and Brecht but also of Sartre. Indeed, as witnessed in the next text, the belated homage that is his detailed analysis of Sartre's play *The Condemned of Altona*, Badiou's earliest ideal as a young writer and student was to become a novelist, playwright, and militant intellectual along the lines of what eventually brought the author of the *Critique of Dialectical Reason* himself to rally to the young Maoists of *La Cause du Peuple*.

Finally, as the English-language reader is gradually gaining access to the texts themselves, with at least two plays recently published in translation, Badiou's own work as a playwright – the author of the novel-opera *L'Écharpe rouge* ('The Red Scarf'), the four published comedies of the Ahmed cycle, and *L'Incident d'Antioche* ('The Incident of Antioch') – forms the topic of the last two texts in the present volume. Thus, in the Ahmed Tetralogy and 'Three Questions to the Author' Badiou both retraces his own extended personal itinerary in relation to the French theatre world and explains the hopes and expectations that he has for the renewal of a genuinely emancipatory, technically masterful, and generically innovative theatre. Such would be the duty of theatre today, as Badiou also writes in his 'Theses on Theater': 'To offer our own time the equivalent of the slaves and domestics of ancient comedy – excluded and invisible people who, all of a sudden, by the effect of the theater-idea, embody upon the stage intelligence and force, desire and mastery.' Far from bemoaning the 'crisis' or 'death' of theatre, this means recapturing the inventive power proper to the stage: 'An invention that would communicate, through theater-ideas, everything of which a people's science is *capable*. We want a theater of capacity, not of incapacity.'[14]

14. Badiou, 'Theses on Theater', pp. 74–5.

1

RHAPSODY FOR THE THEATRE: A SHORT PHILOSOPHICAL TREATISE

I

It is as good a division of the world as any other to observe that there are and have been societies with theatre and others without theatre. And that in societies that know this strange public place, where fiction is consumed as a repeatable event, this has always met with reticence, anathema, major or minor excommunications, as well as enthusiasm. More specifically, next to the spiritual suspicion that befalls theatre, there is always the vigilant concern of the State, to the point where all theatre has been one of the affairs of the State and remains so to this day!

Who fails to see that this territorial and mental division has the additional merit of cutting across that other, all-too-saturated divide of West and East or of North and South? Because at the far end of this East we find the brilliance of a theatre of exception, whereas it is generally elided from Islam. I say 'generally' because no consideration of universal theatricality can ignore the sacred dramas through which Iranian Shi'ism conferred Presence upon its founding martyr.

In this last case, the scandal is home to a heresy. But all true Theatre is a heresy in action. I have the habit of calling its orthodoxy 'theatre': an innocent and prosperous ritual, from which Theatre detaches itself as a rather implausible lightning bolt.

II

Another observation to set things in motion: if cinema is everywhere, it is no doubt because it requires no spectator, only the walls surrounding a viewing public. Let's say that a spectator is real, whereas a viewing public is merely a reality, the lack of which is as full as a full house, since it is only a matter of counting. Cinema counts the viewers, whereas theatre counts on the spectator, and it is in the absence of either one or the other that critics, in a disastrous paradox, invent the spectator of a film and the viewer of a play. François Truffaut deciphers the spectator in the chandelier, but this chandelier is the opposite of the movie projector.

III

I once saw Guy Debord's complete cinematographic oeuvre (which, significantly, had been published in book form) projected without pause, centred on the superb *In girum imus nocte et consumimur igni* (1978), indifferent to the emptiness as much as to the fullness (not of the chandelier but of the seat) in a movie theatre in Paris. This was made possible by the grace of the friendship of Gérard Lebovici, whom killers have since then found it in themselves to shoot down (the man behind such an idea of friendship in art, it must be said regardless of all other considerations, is at once a bit suspect for those who traffic in shadows). This pure temporal moment speaks to the glory of cinema, which may very well survive us humans. It is utterly foreign to theatre, which does not take place without spectators, since in this last case the representation (a word that we will put to the test at length) changes over into a supplementary rehearsal – the exact opposite of those 'dress rehearsals' and other 'final run-throughs' that, through a bit too much of the spectator's real, turn into the premature event of the spectacle's already having taken place.

IV

In the midst of the 'red years', around 1971–2, a group dedicated to cultural intervention, the Groupe Foudre, took it upon itself to cause a racket against the first outbursts of the 'revisionist' malady in the reassessment of the World War II. Movies such as *Lacombe Lucien*[1] or *Night Porter*[2] turned the equivocation between victim and executioner into a fiction, all the while making criminal choices seem innocent. Since then, we certainly have seen where all this would lead. The Groupe Foudre thus readily went to shout down and interrupt those disquieting tripes. Ah, to think of the charming lightness, the polemical health of that era! The watchword invented at the time was: 'Down with the obscurantism of the obscure rooms!' The mistake consisted in ignoring the fact that obscurantism can only be public and that cinema, unlike theatre, is by no means a public

1. *Translator's Note*: *Lacombe Lucien* (1974) is a film directed by Louis Malle.

2. *Translator's Note*: *Il portiere di notte* (1974) is a film by Italian director Liliana Cavani.

place, even if it appears to be one. What is wrapped in obscurity is the private individual, to whom after all we cannot deny the right to obscurity just like that. It is useless to intervene in cinema, because there is no spectator to be found, and, by logical consequence, no public. Being a private industry, cinema is *also* a private spectacle. The time of projection is that of an inconsistent gathering, a serial collection. Cinema, disconnected from the State, proposes no collective signification. The Groupe Foudre was justified in its polemic, full of joy in its action (ah! the ink squirts against the screen on which the colonial paratroopers were strutting, all worked up by the awful John Wayne, in that abomination titled *The Green Berets*!), but it was mistaken in the choice of its site: theatre alone is tied to the State, cinema belongs only to Capital. The former oversees the Crowd, the latter disperses individuals. Cultural–political intervention, which was what the Groupe Foudre dreamed of, has only one possible destination: the theatre. In any case, even here it risks becoming theatricalized rather than politicized.

V

So theatre is an affair of the State, which is morally suspicious, and requires a spectator. That much we know.

We would be better guided in all this, I will say it once and for all, if we relied on a systematic use of François Regnault's *The Spectator,* which is a nearly complete treatise on modern theatre.[3] His guide would give us

3. *Translator's Note*: See François Regnault, *Le Spectateur* (Paris: Beba, 1986). A close friend of Badiou's, Regnault was also invited to give two talks in the conference cycle 'Les Conférences du Perroquet'. Both of these talks dealt with theatre. See François Regnault, *Le Visiteur du soir: Comment peut-on parler d'un spectacle?* (Paris: Le Perroquet, 1985); and *Petite éthique pour le comédien* (Paris: Le Perroquet, 1992).

a different outlook from mine: the outlook of the man of the theatre, which is what Regnault is and which I am not.

The Spectator: point of the real by which a spectacle comes into being and which, as Regnault tells us, corresponds to the taciturn and haphazard evening visitor.

VI

Unless we have recourse to Mallarmé, whose famous Book (as we know from the calculations with which he, like a dreamy apothecary, enumerated the necessary attendants) after all had the form of a Representation.

Mallarmé claims that in his time (but ours is worth as little as his) there is nothing historically real, for lack of a self-declared political collective, and, consequently, that it is theatre that gathers whatever is available to us in terms of action. Here are, in his own style, the two axioms which, for any contemporary thinking of theatre, it would suffice to clarify and meditate upon:

- There is no such thing as a present, for lack of a Crowd's declaring itself.
- Action does not go beyond the Theatre.

Let me add the lesson from Regnault that within him, the Spectator, resides the self-declared Crowd and the untranscendable Action. To him everything is devoted.

VII

Theatre thus distinguishes itself according to the State, of which it is an affair (but why?), according to Morality, for which it is a suspect (but why?), and according to the Spectator, from whom it derives its point of the real, namely, *that which interrupts the rehearsals*. In this last regard, the essence of theatre lies in the existence of the opening night. The fact that there is a second night, so feared by the actors, touches upon the State. That there is a third presupposes that Morality did not prevent it from happening....

But, at the same time, theatre is made up of nothing of the kind. For theatre is a material, corporeal, machinic assemblage. How do those majestic instances (the State, Morality, the Public) come to attach themselves to the scattered and nomadic matter of such an outrageously artisanal operation? What? Some scraps of paper, some rags, a small lamp, three chairs, and a sweet talker from the *banlieues*, and you are ready to claim that public power, morals, and the collective are put on hold, if not endangered?

You better begin by the strict enumeration of the 'parts of the theatre', in the same way that Aristotle spoke of the 'parts of animals'. Show me the animal before concluding, like some abridged Mallarmé, as to its 'superior essence'.[4]

VIII

Let's posit that there is theatre as soon as we can enumerate: first, a public gathered with the intent of a spectacle; second, actors who are physically present, with their voices and bodies, in a space reserved for them with the express purpose of the gathered public's consideration; and, third, a referent, textual or traditional, of which the spectacle can be said to be the representation.

---

4. *Translator's Note*: Mallarmé had written: 'Le Théâtre est d'essence supérieure' ('Theatre is of superior essence'). See Stéphane Mallarmé, *Œuvres*, ed. Henri Modor and Georges Jean-Aubry (Paris: Gallimard, 1945), p. 312.

The third condition excludes mime and dance from being considered theatre, at least when they make up the entire spectacle; it also excludes pure and unrepeatable improvisation. These are theatrical exercises or ingredients, but they are not theatre.

The second condition is incompatible with the idea of a theatre of objects, or with the purely mechanical production of words. A tape recorder can figure onstage, as we see in Jean-Paul Sartre's *The Condemned of Altona* or, better yet, in Samuel Beckett's *Krapp's Last Tape*. However, it is the interlocution between actor and machine that makes for theatre. The machine in and of itself could hardly provide for that.

The first condition excludes that we pretend to be doing theatre by way of the simple theatricalization, out on the streets or indoors, of life as it is. We require a special convocation and a willingness to respond. That there is the need for a public prohibits the idea of theatre for nobody, but not of theatre for a single person, since the latter, as soon as she enters the place of theatre and takes her seat, constitutes a gathering unto herself.

IX

But now onto this elementary description another one superimposes itself, as if theatre were isomorphic with that singular activity we call 'politics' (I am not talking here about the monotonous administration of the State).

In fact, we could argue that there is politics when three things form a knot: the masses who all of a sudden are gathered in an unexpected consistency (events); the points of view incarnated in organic and enumerable actors (subject-effects); a reference in thought that authorizes the elaboration of discourse based upon the mode in which the specific actors in question are held together, even at a distance, by the popular consistency to which chance summons them.

The third point separates politics from everything that is merely blind fury or a nondiscursive impulse. The latter is only the material for politics, not its essence. The social as such is not politics, even if it may be required; nor is the institutional dimension, when taken separately, or the national as the instinct for a place or for an identity.

The second point refuses the existence of a politics that would be unanimous, undivided, monolithic. All existing politics organizes a scission. There is no non-partisan politics.

The first point, inversely, excludes that a reasonable play of institutions alone would be political. For politics to happen, a haphazard point of the real is needed that is revealed by the dispersion abruptly introduced into that which, on the part of the State, ordinarily rules over the general passivity, the symbolic invisibility, of the real of History.

Public, actors, text-thought: would politics be that for which History is only the stage? Is this too romantic an idea? We must come to understand the effects of these axioms, all the while observing in passing that Mallarmé's axioms already engaged both the (missing) Crowd and the (restricted) Action.

X

Of the three elementary conditions of theatre (public, actors, textual referent), which are transcendental or a priori conditions, we can infer a large number of consequences.

The first condition suffices to impose the need for a stage set. A bare arena surrounded by the public turns this public itself into the theatre's setting. If the scene adopts the Italian style, any backdrop serves as a decor, no matter how desolate. When, in Peter Stein's direction of the opening of the *Eumenides*, the priest of Apollo paints the background panel white, he designates the pure act of a stage setting.

From the fact that there is at least one actor we infer that there must be at least one costume. Nudity is no exception, whether it be insignificant (as is often the case) or saturated with meaning.

The existence of a referent, textual or other, constrains the stage director, even if he or she is reduced to continuing a tradition, to the position of director of the company, of a 'self-governed' collective, or the one who, marking the opening beats, guarantees that all the elements come together at the right hour.

Place, text or its placeholder, stage director, actors, decor, costumes, and public are the seven required elements of theatre.

XI

The theatre-politics isomorphism is not limited to this list alone. Indeed, the three obligations of any politics (massive event, organizations, text-thoughts), too, have regulated consequences.

The first is that the State is the inevitable setting of politics. For it is the State's subsistence, its dissemination or its sudden aleatory appearance, that orders the masses of chance. Politics has its origin in this visible event of the State's being given a final notice for proving its legitimacy once more. Some element of the symbolic is struck here, because it becomes manifest that its universality is purely contingent. This unpredictable visibility of the State as separate from the situation and perhaps illegitimate is the horizon for the unfolding of the crowds.

From the second obligation (all politics is organized) we can deduce that politics is never without the efficacy of proper names, those of the political leaders. The body and voice of these actors as the ultimate concentration of organic divisions – all politics exists against other politics – are crucial operators. The death of one of them, for example, suspends the course of events, whether for a long time or for a brief while. Interminable agony, murder or abdication are the principal and unavoidable figures. What the political leader proffers in one tone or another sums up the causalities despite the illusion that it is he who administers them.

The political leader is a visible thought: that by which politics, beneath everything it represents, touches upon presentation itself, and thus upon Being and its truth (just as in theatre the actor finds support in an ethics of play in which some truth scintillates and is eclipsed).

Finally, the third obligation, the one involving referents and texts, includes in political action the historicized function of discourse and its nominal servants, the dead thinkers, in their arrested correlation with a given sequence of real politics.

XII

It belongs no doubt to the singularity of Marxism to have posed that thinkers, referents, and actors should fuse and this, ultimately, on the scale of the masses, just as it proposed to have done with the distinction between the legislative and the executive. In this regard the three obligations seem to add up to only one. This is because Marxism is the politics of a certain end of politics.

There has been a theatre of the end of theatre. It was convivial and potentially orgiastic. But theatre and politics continue: they can exist or not, but they cannot come to an end.

XIII

So: place, text, director, actors, decor, costumes and public are the elements, deducible a priori, of theatre. And organizations, textual referents, thinkers, proper names, the State, contrasting points of view, and evental[5] masses are the obligatory ingredients of a political situation.

These ingredients do not realize themselves in an effective politics except in their fidelity to an event. They do not authorize us to represent politics as something permanent. Politics *takes place,* from time to time. It begins, it ends. And, similarly, from the fact that a theatre production requires the simultaneous and ordered presence of the seven elements, it follows (and this is an essential triviality) that a theatrical spectacle begins and ends. Representation *takes place.* It is a circumscribed event. There can be no permanent theatre. That adjective belongs to cinema, and at the most, to exhibitions. The fact that immediately the spectacle is played a second time changes nothing in this regard. It is two times One, with no access whatsoever to any permanence.

Finally, a spectacle is itself perishable by nature. It can certainly be repeated a good number of times. However, everything in it, or almost everything, is mortal. The

---

5. *Translator's Note*: 'Evental', in spite of the awkwardness of the neologism, has become the quasi-official translation of Badiou's *événementiel* in French. It refers to the site, nature, and consequences of an event in the sense elaborated most systematically in Badiou's *Being and Event*.

seven elements are destined to disperse themselves, and in the end all that is left is the textual referent, which is not theatre in and of itself but at best an exhortation to give it existence.

XIV

The complete temporal precariousness of theatre – which is more easily grasped than that of politics for which the State's nearly atemporal solidity offers some premature consolation – is disquieting to playwrights and directors alike.

The former, especially over the last century, multiply the stage directions for the decor, the interpretation, the gestures, and the costumes, as if to fix *ne varietur* in the textual referent the essence of these other elements. Not even the public escapes their prescriptions: Jean Genet describes its variants in the foreword to *The Blacks*, and, in his projects for the presentation of the Book, Mallarmé manically enumerated its dispositions. The theatre would like to write not only a play but its representation. Though understandable, this desire is in vain. Theatre, which requires writing, never ceases to unwrite itself.[6] Like the piece, the theatre author too is always played.

Stage directors are sometimes distressed by this impermanence. They would like either for the Drama barely to take place – as Mallarmé says, 'the time to show its defeat, which unfolds in a flash'[7] – or else, as Bob Wilson

6. *Translator's Note*: Badiou is playing on Lacan's own pun to define the real as *ce qui ne cesse pas de ne pas s'écrire*, literally 'that which does not cease not to write itself', and *ne cesse pas de s'écrire*, or 'does not cease to write itself', which in turn is a play on *le nécessaire*, 'the necessary'.

7. *Translator's Note:* See sheet 4(A) in the manuscript of Mallarmé's Book reproduced in Jacques Scherer, *Le 'Livre' de Mallarmé* (Paris: Gallimard, 1957).

attempted, for it to last indefinitely. However, neither the eclipse nor the contemplative consistency of pure duration saves theatre from its extended finitude, from its long shortness. No art is so little a κτῆμα ἐς αἰεί (an *everlasting possession* or a *treasure forever*).

At the same time, no other art form is able to pin down the intensity of what happens the way theatre does.

XV

But are you going to tell us finally what is implied by your extended analogy between theatre and politics? That politics is theatre? You announced that this conclusion is too romantic to hold up.

Yes, because it is rather the opposite that is the case. It is true that holding a meeting in the midst of riots is essentially theatrical, even down to the details. Everything, though, works in the other direction: it is theatre, in the circle of its provisional repetition, that figures the knotted components of politics.

Theatre is the figurative reknotting of politics, and this regardless of its subject matter.

Based on this turn of perspective, you should study the difficulty of making theatre out of real politics. Putting Lenin or Mao onstage never goes very far. Büchner's Robespierre is in my eyes a dreamlike fiction that might as well be called Dujardin or Bassompierre.

Evidently, Caesar or Alexander will be more convenient: as ancient conquerors, they can be assimilated to Apollo or to Theseus.

If you wish to obtain the figurative reknotting of politics, take the legend, or that legendary treasure of historical anecdotes that is Plutarch. Because for the others, politics itself provides for its own presentation as well as for its representation.

XVI

Neither the isomorphism with politics (keeping in mind the distance of figuration) nor the list of seven elements identifies theatre in its being. We know since Plato that no list is enough to define an essence, and no analogy amounts to an Idea.

The philosopher will be forgiven for providing a few clarifying barbarisms. Let's call *analytic* of theatre that which concerns the assemblage of the seven elements. Let's call *dialectic* of theatre the singular need for a *spectator* to be summoned to appear in the tribunal of a *morality* under the watchful eye of the *State*. I would say that the aim of the conceptual series whose plot I am anticipating consists in discovering, here and now, the *generic nature* of theatre, meaning that which the traversing of its elements (analytic) by an evental occurrence of its challenge (dialectic) can produce in terms of truth.

If one prefers to *see:* it's a question of thinking the correlation between the two columns in the following table:

THEATRE	
Analytic (elements)	*Dialectic (at-play)*
Place Text	State (situation of the representation)
Director Actor Decor	Ethics of the play (provocation of the presentation)
Costumes Public	Spectator (possible support of Truth)

The productive assemblage of the elements of the analytic is (or is not) the event from which proceed a few truths, by the diagonal movement of the figures of the dialectic.[8]

A representation is then the inquiry into the truth of which the spectator is the vanishing subject.

XVII

If we had to find some order in the following fragments of thought, perhaps it could be the traditional one, in three parts, according to the articulations of the dialectic:
1. Theatre as an affair of the State. I would say that, being at ease with princes and having been founded in the regime of democracy on the agora, theatre is now indecisive, or hurting – not because of the reign of television, as people pretend, but due to the essential lack of politics in which the electoral process is resolved. Theatre, therefore, is sick of parliaments and cared for by unions of all kinds as one is cared for onstage by Molière's doctors (we will posit that the Ministry of Culture is part of the unions).

As art: theatre undoes the bonds of political desire with great virtuosity but it cannot accommodate the social, even though it is forced to do so.

8. *Translator's Note*: Badiou's usage of the term 'dialectic' to refer to a movement that diagonally cuts across and at the same time activates a static list of elements, here called 'analytic', is not uncommon in his philosophical work. For instance, he similarly opposes 'dialectic' and 'combinatory' in *Théorie de la contradiction* (Paris: Maspero, 1975) and 'dialectical' and 'structural' in *Theory of the Subject*, trans. Bruno Bosteels (London: Continuum, 2009). Here, in interpreting the diagram, the reader might want to consider how the effects of the theatre-event that is the always-singular performance of the spectacle pick up on the constitutive elements of the 'analytic' so as to produce the higher concepts of the 'dialectic': the three terms in the right-hand column thus can be said to traverse the seven elements from the left-hand column, even though this movement itself is almost by definition not visualized in the diagram.

2. Theatre as the putting at stake [*enjeu*] of an ethics – and first of all of an ethics of play [*jeu*], so rare and deeply moving. I would say that, accustomed by the comic to pronounce that what has worth is only semblance, by the tragic that what saves is also what brings perdition, theatre has a hard time breathing from the moment that this semblance has value and all salvation lies in flight, which is the nonspirit of our times.
3. Theatre as the eclipse and impact of at least one spectator. This time we must tackle the public (or its notion, not its number, or its existence). Hyperbolically, the public is affected, or infected, by laziness, which is the only vice that theatre (which knows them all) cannot accommodate, and this precisely because it must please, and purge, the passions. No effect of truth, not even that of scenic sumptuousness, can purge the lazy of their passion, which is ignorance.

Or, as Antoine Vitez[9] used to tell me – theatre having taught him this profound truth: the essence of vulgarity, even the worst kind that is that of the executioner, is laziness, that is, wanting to 'live' without working or thinking.

XVIII

Yes, in the end, this is what gives me pleasure: that to speak of Theatre today, cornered as it is between the Ministry and the world of 'cultural' entertainment, obliges us to write a sort of manifesto against the lazy.

---

9. *Translator's Note*: Antoine Vitez was the French director who headed the National Theatre of Chaillot and later the Comédie-Française, and who sought to create a popular theatre without condescending populism, an 'elite theatre for all'. His ideas for the theatre can be found in the anthology Antoine Vitez, *Le Théâtre des idées*, ed. Danièle Sallenave and Georges Banu (Paris: Gallimard, 1991). For Badiou's personal relation to Vitez, see 'The Ahmed Tetralogy', below.

Every productivist society probably counts intellectual laziness, the loathing of thought, as its dominant passion (Lacan was the first to identify this passion, in correlation with hatred and love, as the passion of ignorance).

The impasse of theatre allows us to devise a *disorientation* of laziness. Or to confront it with its mirror image. Spectator! You are this precious point where thought becomes velvet, shadow, silence.

Theatre can *show* the ugliness of the lazy person (one will point the projector at his briefcase, at all the emblems of his unending work of laziness, his infinite and exhausting labour which is only meant to ensure that, at the supreme point of time, thinking comes to lack).

The aridity of theatre as a mirroring glacier in which, having arrived in all innocence at the evenings of Culture, the lazy (the intellectual? the cadre? Woman? the critic?) becomes visible to us as the coalescence of himself and that which, through money, leads everywhere to the extinction of all fire.

XIX

THE EMPIRICIST: There is also laziness in your way of proceeding. You give yourself the luxury of heightening the brilliance of the event, the precarious, the scintillating, but all you do is pile up concepts. This is dogmatic slumber.

ME: What do you want? Some examples? Some spectacles? Some frozen Eskimos?

THE EMPIRICIST: That you take some risks, here and now.

ME: Show me the battlefield.

THE EMPIRICIST: You oppose 'theatre', the mere analytical combination of seven elements....

ME: I've said nothing of the kind, at least not until now.

THE EMPIRICIST: But I can predict you. So to this 'theatre' you oppose Theatre, which puts in motion the dialectic – the 'diagonal', you say in your jargon – of the State, of Ethics, and of the Spectator (the subject). Tell me, here and now, what is 'theatre'? And Theatre? Why not distribute a few points, good ones and bad ones, so that we gain some clarity.

ME: Do you authorize me to give one last dissertation?

THE EMPIRICIST: Only if it is related to my challenge.

ME: It's about the link between 'theatre' and private property!

THE EMPIRICIST: So now you go for vulgar Marxism! Base and superstructure! You are making fun of people!

ME: Give me a chance.

THE EMPIRICIST: As soon as you're done with your dissertation, you will give me a concrete list of real spectacles from the past ten years that in your eyes are Theatre and not 'theatre'.

ME: That's not out of the question.

THE EMPIRICIST: Dogmatic but prudent. Well then, go ahead.

XX

There exists a private, prosperous, and continuous theatre. It is faithfully multiplied by television (Masterpiece Theatre). It provides cinema with innumerable and triumphant adaptations. Between its stage and the screens of all formats, there is an uninterrupted circulation of dialogues, plot lines, roles, and actors. It balances its budgets without need for subsidies. It is called 'boulevard theatre', but we cannot decide whether this appellation does wrong to the theatre or to the boulevards. From Jean de Létraz[10] to Harold Pinter, it has its nuances, its high and its low classes, like cars. In its own way, it is complete, and most often that is also how it appears on the posters, as completely sold out, contrary to many national, regional, or municipal theatres.

What is interesting is that this theatre counts for nothing. This is by no means evident from the facts. With regard to the link between Culture and the State, the problems of representation and the unions, the aporias of form, the scandals of meaning, or the despotic surveillance, this theatre is as lowly as the current film industry. Applauded by the shopkeeping bourgeoisie, greasy like pork and beans, conventional like an *Ave Maria* telephoned in by actors whose only effect lies in tremor or slow motion, many of the spectacles of this private circuit are in their own genre more well-rounded, more put together, and better packaged than many of the cadaverous 'creations' of the cultural circuit, not to mention the butchering of the classics, which the good intentions of modernization leave raw-boned and opaque – I am thinking of those *Cid* and *Athalie* from my youth performed for the high-school matinées, which in themselves would be enough to draw some crucial lessons, to be engraved on their tombstones, about the connection of the State to pedagogy, the boards of trustees, the classical repertoire, theatre productions in the style of *Captain Fracasse,*[11] and the capacity of schoolkids to turn a ceremony into a riot. However, these comparisons are pointless, precisely because they only seem to function among genres, whereas in reality they compare

10. *Translator's Note*: A popular dramatist and TV writer, Jean de Létraz was also director of the Théâtre du Palais-Royal (1942–54).

11. *Translator's Note*: Originally a novel by Théophile Gaultier, *Captain Fracasse* is an adventure tale, full of sword fights and romantic drama, which has been adapted to film and theatre repeatedly.

one kind of place to another. Private, cut out from the conversations overseen by *Le Nouvel Observateur*,[12] forbidden among teachers (and, furthermore, unworthy and repugnant indeed, but that is not what matters), the boulevard is destatified, deunionized, a bad object of theatre, a false theatre, 'theatre' for laughs. Tied to the State, a reference point for opinionating, mediated by credit, budgets, and institutions, dignified and devoted to the instruction of the crowds, public theatre – national, regional, departmental (like the muse), or municipal – organizes a subject-spectator who is juridically cultural, even if empirically hollow. The theatre of meaning wants a minister, that is, subsidies for the cultural surveillance by the republican State. The theatre of the boulevard, the theatre of indecency, can desire only obscene revenues.

XXI

THE EMPIRICIST: Knock yourself out.

ME: One other dissertation, just one! It directly concerns our topic. It is about Theatre and 'theatre'. Let me return to the Good and the Bad, before giving out good and bad points.

THE EMPIRICIST: The Good is only the common feature of all things good; the Bad of all things bad. How do we go from the Good to the good? There is Theatre only insofar as there are spectacles of Theatre, and 'theatre', insofar as there are spectacles of 'theatre'.

ME: Indulge my taste for the a priori one more time.

THE EMPIRICIST: OK, but this is the last time.

12. *Translator's Note*: *Le Nouvel Observateur* is a liberal weekly news magazine in France.

XXII

I call Theatre, without quotation marks, a production that conjures the seven constitutive elements of every analytic of Theatre (or of 'theatre' as well, since analysis cannot make this distinction) in such a way as to pronounce itself about itself and about the world, and such that the knot of this double examination summons the spectator at the impasse of a form of thought.

By contrast, there is a 'theatre' that is fulfilling, a 'theatre' of established meanings, a 'theatre' from which nothing is lacking and which, abolishing chance, induces a convivial satisfaction in those who hate truth. This 'theatre', which is the inversion of Theatre, can be recognized in the fact that those who come to exhibit their salacious or restrained enjoyment in it are marked by an identitarian sign, be it constituted by class or by opinion. The true public of true Theatre, by contrast, is generic, by which I mean an indiscernible and atypical subtraction from what Mallarmé calls the Crowd. Only a Crowd can make a Spectator, in the sense designated by François Regnault, that is, someone who exposes him or herself, in the distance of a representation, to the torment of a truth. We should therefore say the following: complicit with certain representations, certain publics manifest their hatred of Theatre by the fervour of their attending 'theatre'.

XXIII

There exists a specific hatred of Theatre, which every soul is capable of. Theatre is of all the art forms the most hated, under the cover of the adoration devoted to 'theatre'. There are times when one would want to break one's seat out of rage and hatred, when one would throw oneself out onto the boulevard to find consolation from so much torment and effort.

Fortunately, there is little, very little Theatre, because 'theatre' most often protects us from it. As is the case of today's politics, isomorphous to every collective instance of thought in the fixed time and material place of an intervention, Theatre has almost vanished, so that it is extremely difficult to discover it and to sustain it.

Just as the parliamentary form of politics, that commodity without concept, by virtue of the thickness of the consensus it organizes renders almost invisible and untenable all genuine politics capable of thinking at the locale where it takes place, so too does the omnipresence of 'theatre' dissimulate the elevated, superior exigency of Theatre.

XXIV

And yet, theatre exists – as does politics. I will say that theatre is possible. It is to this possibility that we will speak when we remark upon the vigilant hatred that theatre provokes in critics and the public, and upon the unceasing effort to suppress its conditions.

Here, 'conditions' is a stronger term than 'elements', in the sense of the analytic (the seven elements: place, text, director, actor, decor, costumes, public). 'Conditions' means the elements but renamed in their tension, their prescription, their difficulty. These elements render possible *today* the dialectic of the theatrical State, the ethics of play, and the subject-spectator.

We could make this sur-nomination of the elements operative by saying: there is Theatre (and not 'theatre') only in the conjunction of the following elements: the text it elicits and thus makes contemporary; the division it effects; the haphazard thought of a stage director for whom this text – I am picking up an expression from Antoine Vitez – becomes the filter of a divination; actors capable of unfolding the real point of departure that they and they alone constitute, rather than showing off the rhetorics of body and voice; and at least one spectator.

Under these conditions, it is possible that we come upon the process of a truth, of an elucidation whose spectacle would be the event. Consequently, hatred will manifest itself for sure, due to the fact that it is properly impossible simply to watch what happens there. Because under these conditions, theatre makes it known to you that you will not be able innocently to remain *in your place.*

XXV

The hatred of Theatre, expressed in the love of 'theatre', is ultimately a form of self-hatred. We are that person who arrived for the sake of the ritual insipidness of a celebration of self, some laughs, culture, recognizable figures, feeling always one foot ahead, answers that 'hit the nail on the head', sublime decor, communion during intermission. All of a sudden, sticking closely to the event's unfolding and following a set of trajectories subtracted from all calculation, we must pass through the twists and turns of desire, see the object eclipse itself before our eyes and, in the impasse of form, hit upon some incongruous point of the real. In order not to endure all this in a disagreeable commotion, and so as not to avoid it through the facile solution of boredom, there is no resource other than a willful attention and a sustained, though latent, exercise of thinking.

The paradox of theatre, which exposes it to hatred, lies in the fact that it presents itself as a figurative luxury, a solid chain, a cultural temple, but unless it is 'theatre' it is actually made of flight and chance – a difficult art, one that is especially intellectual, whose spectator is the empty point from where the fragile instant of a thought proceeds, if it is not the nothing that exists as boredom. So much apparent or promised beauty for such an aleatory effort! The hatred of Theatre stems from the presence of some snare in this sensible arrangement of bodies, voices, and images that takes on meaning by fugaciously giving brilliance to the unassignable cause of a truth. It is as if a mathematical demonstration – and theatre is more demonstrative than representative – were announced to you for the purpose of the enjoyment of its fruits.

It also so happens that the idea of spectacle is commonly associated – any cinema, 'theatre', the opera that is 'in' or the big show all converge upon this conviction – with a certain unanimous passivity, with being captured in the energy of the image or the divine voice. But Theatre demands that its spectator, who as a result will feel the hardness of his seat, attach the development of meaning to the lacunae of the play, and that he become in turn the interpreter of the interpretation. Who would not detest the fact of having paid for pleasure and being forced to perform a kind of work? Or rather, who would not hate that this pleasure, which one would desire to be immediate, is the doubtful product of the mind's concentrated effort?

XXVI

The truths lavished by the labour of theatre are essentially political in that they crystallize the dialectics of existence and aim to elucidate our temporal site.

To be more exact: of all the arts, theatre is the one

that most insistently stands *next to* (or supposes) politics. I have already shown:

- the existence of a formal analogy between politics and theatre
- the implication of the State in the essence of theatre

It is true that this analogy and this implication apply to 'theatre' as much as to Theatre. But the latter makes an event out of the *saying*, in a torsion, of this analogy and this implication.

'Theatre' is *of* the State, though it has nothing to say about this. It perpetuates and organizes the easygoing and grumpy subjectivity that is needed for the State.

Theatre, for its part, always *says* something about the State, and finally about the state (of the situation). There are certainly good reasons for not wanting to listen to this saying.

XXVII

THE EMPIRICIST: My lists, my lists! You won't escape any longer.

ME: I am far from having seen everything.

THE EMPIRICIST (*unforgiving*):
If you thought it was Theatre, and not 'theatre', you would have gone to see it.

ME: No, there is such a thing as chance, laziness....

THE EMPIRICIST (*ferocious*):
You said that theatre is a war machine against laziness.

ME: There is the press, the time needed, forgetfulness. I am going to be unfair.

THE EMPIRICIST (*cynical*):
So be it.

ME: Since when? Forty years?

THE EMPIRICIST: That's it! To celebrate only the living, and omit only the dead. No, no. I want your theatre spectacles from the last ten years.

ME: Well then, a restricted, minimalist, essential list.

THE EMPIRICIST: No precautions.

ME (*in one go*): Wagner's *Tetralogy* directed by Chéreau-Boulez in Bayreuth; Ibsen's *Peer Gynt,* by Chéreau; Aeschylus' *Oresteia,* by Peter Stein; Racine's *Bérénice,* by Vitez; and *Bérénice* by Grüber; *Phèdre* by Stein; Guyotat's *Tomb for 500,000 Soldiers,* by Vitez; Marivaux's *Triumph of Love,* in Italian, by Vitez; Goldoni's *Harlequin, Servant of Two Masters,* by Strehler; and.... No, I stop here. I should above all apologize for not naming the actors. It is always necessary to name the actors, and the stage designers, and the costume designers, and the musicians, if there are any.

THE EMPIRICIST: Only one contemporary author! Aeschylus, Racine, Marivaux, Goldoni! Such academicism!

ME (*in one go*): Bernard-Marie Koltès's *In the Solitude of the Cotton Fields,* by Chéreau; René Kalisky's *Falsch,* by Vitez; and.... No, I stop here. We would have to cite all the attempts. For the contemporary moment, we must support and salute *every* attempt. But, dear empiricist, you've granted me only ten years.

THE EMPIRICIST: And all these spectacles, in the great official temples: Bayreuth, Chaillot, Villeurbanne, the Théâtre Français, the Schaubühne.... Nothing lateral, not one small place, none of the provinces with their supreme discretion. Your 'diagonal' is that of the sumptuous and of Big Credit.

ME: Why is the dimension of the place important? Even if only ten persons went, theatre would persist in incarnating all by itself – for example, against the Ministry of the Police, or of War, or of Artisans and

Commerce – the Ministry of Culture, lending it its living flesh and rendering its minister legitimate or illegitimate. Theatre, under the sign of its national grandeur, is the general union of culture. And since it is clear that this does not depend on its importance – socially very weak today – we are forced to conclude that it belongs to its essence. Theatre is essentially a form of the State.

THE EMPIRICIST: I foresee a new dissertation.

ME: Not at all! It's a memory from my adolescence. From 1953. My father was mayor of Toulouse. He tells of the incidents surrounding the vote on the budget of the municipal council. The mayor's role consists most of the time in skillfully linking the answer 'Motion accepted!' to the question 'No opposition?' – after reading at full speed from a book of magic spells whose emollient and somniferous powers are well demonstrated. The speedy syntagma 'Nooppositionmotionaccepted' is the sesame of the vote. But for one chapter at least, this syntagma malfunctioned: when the theatre budget was announced – the budget for the great and glorious Théâtre du Capitole, loved by Stendhal. Ah! It is as though there had been a clarion call. The council members shake, they snort, they click their heels and throw themselves into an endless quarrel. The discussion turns fussy, twisted, people deliberate the retirement of ushers and the replacement of a chipped harp. Wagner or *La Belle de Cadix*? The question poisons the mood.

For the schools and the hospitals, the public roads, transportation, drinking water and public gardens, 'nooppositionmotionaccepted'. For theatre, inevitably, the sound and the fury. The representations wake up the representatives. Theatre's link to the budget is theatrical rather than budgetary.

THE EMPIRICIST: Finally something concrete!

XXVIII

1965. Mao Zedong, 'China's master', as the newspapers say, proposes with the help of his wife – who is after all an actress – to reform the Beijing Opera. It is a matter of putting an end to the hegemony of aristocrats and warriors, of 'squires and damsels' on the stage (as well as, for quite some time, in reality). Theatre must guarantee the popular triumph of workers, peasants, and soldiers. Of course, we keep the music, we keep the resources of the plot, we keep the good and bad emotions, in reality we keep everything, but for the princes we substitute the heroes of the people's war. It is almost a simple costume change. Well, the affair brought about ten years of bloody tumultuousness; shady political episodes will shake China from the smallest factory in the provinces all the way to the Politburo; and in the end – surprise! – it will fail. Mao wasn't even dead yet when it failed: squires and damsels were back on the stage, much to the relief of Deng Xiaoping, who used to be bored to death by the operas 'with a contemporary revolutionary theme.' To purge theatre of its traditional heroes – kings, princesses, courtesans, elegant ladies and dandies, maids and soothsayers: they are the same everywhere, the affair has nothing particularly Chinese to it – was not within the power of the historical leader of the revolution, not even when supported by twenty million Red Guards, worker factions, and a few army units. Nobody can take the theatre by assault. Theatre is more solidly statelike than the State itself.

XXIX

1982. Antoine Vitez is enraged against the very notion of a 'dramaturge'. This is one of his most constant themes: 'As long as I am alive, he declares, there will be no dramaturge here, except in the sense of the one who writes plays.' The German tradition of the dramaturge in his eyes is that of a policeman of the text who forbids the theatre artist 'on the spot' to seize hold of the scenic situation. The dramaturge introduces a legitimist politics into the theatre, with the director as his technical bag holder. What exasperates Vitez is this separation put in place between the textual exegesis, which produces meaning, and the actual theatrical gesture. This is because, for him, theatre is a form of thought, and there is no thought prior to it except the being of the text, which has no need of anyone, since it is the objective filter of the theatrical intervention.

Vitez is right about this, of course. It is all the more saddening that a cop in charge of meaning becomes involved in rehearsals just as we may conjecture that one cop (at least) in charge of public order will be present in the house. Theatre is essentially under surveillance. It is the possible place of political effects: an *official conspiracy*. In Molière's comedies, in Racine's tragedies, the king himself is made privy, through the exaltation that is proper to art, to the ignoble world in which he participates, to the public conspiracy of his entourage, to the hypocrisies and cruelties of his own power. But his police are on hand to signal to him what might be excessive in this first artistic designation. There will be interdictions, there will be postponements. However, even while being under surveillance, theatre also does some surveillance of its own. It relates the real. It blows the whistle on the world better than any police report could. For this reason the king prefers to be instructed by the theatre, despite the palace intrigues, rather than listen to the bores around him.

Even today, this or that play touching upon Jewish topics, upon large corporations under threat, upon the church or the police, will produce a public effect of scandal and intrigue that no movie can hope for. This is because everything that the theatre pronounces is official in an obscure sense. It is something for which we can hold the authorities accountable. Cinema is capitalist and private. Nobody is responsible for it, other than a producer and his employees. Whatever is said in theatre, even in a schoolyard illuminated by two small lamps, is said *with majesty.* If it is scandalous, it is because the State does not keep watch over itself enough: it does not keep watch over its own words.

XXX

1984. Vitez produces my play from 1978, *The Red Scarf,* in an opera version scored by Georges Aperghis. The spectacle fulfills me. Several friends remark that in the third act, on the open blue space of the stage, the characters going their own way – all of them militants and cadres of a revolutionary adventure whose site and whose Party is invented, all of them taking different paths, torn and displaced, all of them stubborn in their conviction – end up resembling…Greek gods. Thus, it is all well to pile up 'Central Committee', 'proletariat', 'Marxism', 'red flag', 'factory in revolt', 'revolutionary war'; to make all this sing, to tie it to love, to the embrace, to death; to assemble a comic interlude on the dialectic, and another (in a rowboat) between Althusser and Deleuze, more or less. Very well, but all this scares and darkens only the minds of the opera critics and the bourgeoisie in places like Lyon. For the spectator who simply accepts to be one, this story of the communist epic is inscribed in the great categories of myth where theatre, since the beginning, has articulated the effects of politics. It pronounces, in the splendour of the theatre, both that the time of these particular heroes is over and therefore that now comes the time of their scenic sublimation by which the State finally legitimates them, inscribes them on the tablets of the tragic law, and thus puts them to rest in death, in egalitarian fashion, next to Orestes, Creon, Titus, Polyeucte, Ruy Blas, Don Rodrigue – next to Electra, Antigone, Bérénice, Junie, the eternal queens, and Ysé and Isolde. I was already quite surprised that Antoine – the character in my play who, tied to the Russians, or 'revisionist' as we used to say at the time, and enamored only with Europe, was in my eyes, in 1972–3, the incarnation of everything bad – reemerges on stage with a tragic consistency that is only further amplified by its irony. This shows that ideological intentions, even if they govern the lateral construction of consciousness, cannot pretend to control what theatre, as myth or rather mythification whose being is the State, will *discover* in the textual proposition. Thus filtered and dressed up, framed by the red of the stage and bathed in the modernity of song, my play said three things about the 'red years', which go from 1917 to 1977:

- It's over.
- It possessed a beauty that honours our Greek ancestors, in tragedy.
- What it was exactly is a question that we are still charged with.

Indeed, if theatre distinguishes what mythifies from what is in decline in the name of the State, it is not in a position to draw any conclusion. It is the state of affairs put *in abeyance*.

XXXI

1986. People from the theatre world, under the energetic and inventive guidance of Ariane Mnouchkine, organize a powerful demonstration against François Léotard's nomination as Minister of Culture under Chirac. What did he do, the poor simpleton, the baffled Boy Scout? First off, he has less money, like everybody else. As a result, after having guaranteed their seat to all the pontiffs of the major theatres (and with good reason), Léotard imagines that his 'power' as minister, beyond the major conservative obligations (besides, the minister's aid in charge of theatre, Robert Abirached, is still there and will remain there, a pillar of cohabitation), consists in wiping out a few subaltern subsidies. 'But come on! We haven't made the liberal revolution for nothing!' says the handsome hunk from Fréjus[13] to himself. Generalized uproar!

Now, what is the directive behind this melodramatic episode of the class struggle in the theatre? People will march through the streets while shouting the surprising slogan, which is not without a little batrachian aspect: 'We want a minister!'[14] Léotard was accused of not being one, given the modifications in quantity and hierarchy of the handsome payments.

The world-weary will tell me: 'Don't go and look too far. These people bemoaned the Left, they were doing a postelectoral campaign.' Behind 'We want a minister' I certainly hear 'We want Jack Lang', the bouncing Lang

13. *Translator's Note*: Fréjus is a small, provincial town in the south of France and Robert Abirached's place of origin.

14. *Translator's Note*: With the 'batrachian' aspect of this episode as with the 'frogs' in the following paragraph, Badiou is referring to Jean de La Fontaine's fable 'The Frogs Asking a King,' in which the frogs' demand, 'We want a king!', is answered by God's sending a crane that gulps them down at pleasure.

to whom all of cultural France, from the hard rocker in Saint-Gaudens[15] to the manager launching his brand of hip neckties, devotes a cult of recognition. But I maintain the importance of the symptom: no corporation has ever cried in public for obtaining a 'true minister' the way theatre did that day, except perhaps that rather nostalgic bunch of phased retirees and repatriates of our late colonial wars.

XXXII

Quite a few theatres are national. There is the Comédie-Française, obviously, which cost Malraux (now there is a minister, perhaps like the one the cash boxes hoped for, but a military coup d'état doesn't happen every day) a long battle, with a siege, bailiffs, decrees, just to drive out the administrator at the time who was called, as in a play, Monsieur de Boisanger.[16] There is the National Theatre of Chaillot. Even at the time of its exile in Villeurbanne, the Théâtre populaire remained national.

If it is not national, a theatre worthy of this name is at least regional. It is beaming, well established and active in Languedoc-Roussillon or in Poitou-Charentes. It thus remains in close proximity to the limitations and possibilities (above all financial) of the local Assemblies, for lack of the Bourbon Palace.

---

15. *Translator's Note*: Saint-Gaudens is a small town outside of Toulouse, in the South of France. Anecdotally, it is where Badiou often retreats to read and write in the country house passed down by his father, who was Mayor of Toulouse from 1944 to 1958. For a 'phenomenological' description of the effects of another noise, that of a motorbike, for the 'world' of Saint-Gaudens outside this country house, see Book II in Badiou's *Logics of Worlds*.

16. *Translator's Note*: Claude Bréart de Boisanger was the director of the Comédie-Française at the time of Malraux's proposed reforms in 1959.

Like the government for the body of the nation, a theatre will also be a Centre (for drama, culture, creation ...) whose circumference is nowhere. However, this Centre is always a House – a Molière House, which sounds like a cenotaph, or a Cultural House, which sounds like something from a university in the suburbs. In this house, the 'house master and his team' receive the public, feed it, educate it, and of course they hold democratic debates with it. This equivocal relation between the verticality of the Centre and the hospitality of the House is the same one that we find in our current Republic: firm presidential elevation of power, tender economical and pedagogical concern for the governed. Cult of the master (theatre people will not be the last to plead emphatically with the dark and obtuse Mitterrand to reenlist: 'France needs you, and so on', they know the drill) and cult of the public, in an uncertain balance, with the staging of 'public debates' as their farce.

Can one imagine a 'national cinema'? It would produce laughter. A film archive, yes, but everyone knows this is only a museum. Can one imagine a film director as 'house master' interested in receiving the public in his 'house'? A house about which he moreover would have the obligation to tell his hosts, with a phrase typical of republican banquets, that 'it is theirs', or that 'they are at home in it'? Can one imagine a 'beaming' cinema in Languedoc-Roussillon? Cinema is too trivial for the metaphors of the republican State. Crassly mixed up with the capitalist infrastructure, it cannot climb the steps of subvention, from the municipality to the Elysée, nor can it articulate itself, from the basic master of ceremonies to the minister, in terms of cultural demand.

XXXIII

Theatre and the State. The State and Revolution. Theatre and Revolution. I am thinking of the movie *Danton* (1983) by Andrzej Wajda. Drawing from a really beautiful play by the Polish Stanislawa Przybyszewska, who, trained under Mathiez, is a fervent Robespierrist, Wajda gives a rightist turn to the play thanks to a thundering, lewd, and thick Depardieu, demagogue of 'life', who is in fact utterly uninteresting (let's say: an anarcho-desiring union leader of the CFDT[17] from the years 1973–6). By contrast, the Robespierre played by the Polish actor Wojciech Pszoniak, is enthralling, entirely invested and absorbed in the political process. So I ask myself: how come, first of all, that the great theatre of the revolution is so rare (aside from this play, what do we have? Georg Büchner? Romain Rolland, in any case, has failed) and of foreign origin? Is there, furthermore, a truly convincing Russian theatre with 1917 as its subject matter? A Chinese theatre on the sequence 1923–49? There are books, poems, movies, nobody will doubt that. But has the theatre, grand theatre, gone this way? Even the political war that is the subject matter of my *Red Scarf* is a fiction, a dreamlike synthesis. I am afraid that we must conclude that the theatre *avoids* the revolution as the point of the real of politics. It likes the palace intrigues, the successions, the murders, the conspiracies but, always in a metonymical rapport with regard to the crowd, haunted by heroic representation and its irreparable division, it is troubled by the revolution. To the latter it prefers, so to speak, its retrospective premonition (Chekhov) or its legendary reconstruction (the founding of the public tribunal in Aeschylus' *Oresteia*).

17. *Translator's Note*: Confédération Française Démocratique du Travail (French Democratic Confederation of Labour), one of five major French trade unions.

At best, it would mark its time of failure, its disastrous turn, the discussion of its setting sun – as in Sean O'Casey's plays where the conjunction between socialism and the national question inflames a premature youth or toughens the eternal old woman – melancholies of the decision that is also, always, where Brecht's uncertain heroes end up.

This is because in the theatre, in the form of the State, revolution is a matter of failure or success, and thus of death or life; and because in the theatre the existential categories of politics stand eclipsed. Theatre treats not politics but the consciousnesses raised in *the state of politics*. Theatre is confirmed in its statelike vocation by this state-ification of the revolutionary procedure, whose hero is the visible production. Theatre has always treated the revolution as a myth. Let me add in passing that this does not prove that it *was* a myth but only that, in theatre, that part of the revolution that was *not* a myth cannot be represented.

XXXIV

Unable to show the revolution, caught in the habit of the State, is theatre not the only art to establish a certain *visibility* of the State? The only art to show the State? What does the theatre talk about if not the state of the State, the state of society, the state of the revolution, the state of consciousness relative to the State, to society, to the revolution, to politics? To the state of love, too, which is very different from love. (I hold that the novel treats love, but that in the theatre love is an axiom, a condition for tying together a state of affairs, places and people. Nobody loves, onstage; here love is pronounced in terms of its consequences, but we need the novel to escort love itself artistically. In the theatre, love is a declaration to support a strategy, imbued with power. It is not, it cannot be, a generic sentiment.)

Theatre: art of the *declaration of the state* (of affairs). Inventory of all the parts of a closed situation as catastrophe. Final settlement in full, and explosion. The bursting, of tears or of laughter, as end (and as end goal) of the strategic enumeration of the passions and the meetings.

Theatre, indeed, represents: it *represents the representation,* not the presentation. The State, not the emergence of its place. It is the ceremony of all ceremonies. It does not begin until the (political, Greek) freedom to judge the representation is immanent to the conditions of art. It authorizes itself by representing representations. Thus, by the Idea (in Plato's sense). All theatre is a theatre of Ideas.

XXXV

But there is also a law of distortion, characteristic of the stage: being a form of the State, theatre can only show an 'other state' of affairs than the one of which it is a form. Theatre *distances* the State it shows because this showing is informed, put into form, on the basis of the State itself.

XXXVI

Examples: The tragic authors of the era of Greek democracy suppose the presence onstage of unlikely monarchs. The Chorus is certainly an assembly, but it is subordinate. Theatre, conditioned by democracy, aims at it through a legendary monarchical distance. Our tragic authors from the time of absolute monarchy have recourse to Roman emperors, Greek heroes, barbaric kings. They live in the court, but in a faraway discursivity. Our tragic authors from the Restoration, from the era of Louis-Philippe, who are prey to imperial nostalgias and look forward to the republican dream, find a way to balance these vexed dispositions through the Middle Ages, the Renaissance, or the Fronde.[18] Claudel, our poet of the Third Republic, its colonies, its exasperated and absurd patriotism, except for *La Ville,* fashions some hyperbolic Spanish themes, belabours the revolutionary effect, or harkens back to the medieval land. Even the figures of the brothel in Genet's *The Balcony* are drawn from a defunct republic of notables, from a Cross and a Sword that evoke Boulanger rather than Pompidou.[19] And nobody, it must be said, has ever been able to play or put onstage his solar rebel – to the contrary, the unpunished vice of the text excels in supporting, on the stage, the dickhead of the police prefect.

XXXVII

Theatre, which is a form of the State, says what this State *will have been* by lending it the fable of a past. Unable to come back to the present it activates, theatre establishes the future anterior of a state of affairs by putting it at the distance that is required for the present of its operation. Thinking in terms of time, theatre *executes* this thinking in the past tense.

---

18. *Translator's Note*: The Fronde was an era of civil war in France lasting from 1648 to 1653.

19. *Translator's Note*: Georges Ernest Jean-Marie Boulanger (1837–91) was a French general and reactionary politician. Georges Pompidou was president of the Republic during 1969–74.

XXXVIII

I claim that, at this point to which I've brought you, we can go back to the topic of Corneille and Racine. La Bruyère, who affirmed that there was nothing new to be said anymore, also did not say everything new that there is to say about our two tragic authors. (Their distance signifies the whole country, which a narrow and financially cheap Europe invites us to forget. 'European Theatre?' I only know specific theatres, and what I like about them is their dissimilarity, their nonunity. I love England, Germany, Russia, France.... I do not love Europe.)

Corneille and Racine, and thus, France according to its hiatus (and France *is* a hiatus, a conflict, a gap, it is anything but a substance or a union), do not mean, and never have, 'human beings as they should be' versus 'human beings as they are'. I will raise high Corneille's banner, with some bad faith: he still dwells on, gets mixed up in, and equivocates on the passes and impasses of politics. Trained by Richelieu in matters of invention and by the Fronde, in disorder, he still believes that politics exists, that the theme of the good king clarifies its procedure, that the debate is open and complicated – and the old man adds to the mix some superb hysterics, which Racine's ferocious existential misers cannot match. When he comes to understand that all this is over, that nothing happens anymore, that politics has been suppressed for a long time, he maintains the anguished recollection of it in melancholic and suicidal figures, who are sentimental about politics all the while being led astray into the law-without-law of the State. As someone who dreams of a politics in dispute, it is true that Corneille is troubled by the theatre. There is something novelistic that animates and undoes his construction. The amplitude of his discourse, the subjective explanation of the torment of the Idea, the becoming eclipsed of the real, the ungraspable horror of power: in all this there is a whirling that a balanced language captures, returns and indefinitely rebounds into the hall of mirrors of an essential deception.

Racine, the ingenious one, the professional sycophant, situates himself from the start in the nonexistence of politics. He shows no mourning over this. He takes delight in arranging its lack in the combinatory laws of power and desire. He observes the spiders in their jar, and, through the most perfect and precise language ever fashioned, he calculates their trajectories and their encounters. The cruelty of the State, its pure point of the real, the weakness of the vanquished, the watchful eye of the victors, the cause of desire, the evanescent complacency of love, all this is as though exhibited in a diamond cutter's montage. But at bottom, what do we care? What soul is educated here about what? Too much of the real is overburdening.

Corneille, in order to defend his chimerical constructions, often follows Boileau's statement: 'The true sometimes may not be likely'.[20] Better yet, or worse: The true is *never* likely. Corneille searches for a theatre of truth, Racine for one of the real. That is the crux of the question: human beings as they are *in truth*, and human beings as they are, period.

Theatre in which the state of affairs is said in the shortest indirect manner: theatre of language and of desire (Racine). Theatre in which the political idea seeks to unravel the unreasonable grasp of the State: theatre of discourse and of truth (Corneille).

Racine, certainly, more perfect, as far as the theatre is concerned. The other, often on the verge of the unplayable. Racine at-play [*en-jeu*], Corneille disingenuously

20. *Translator's Note*: Nicholas Boileau (1636–1711) was a French poet and critic known for his insistence on classical standards.

out-played [*in-jeu-nu*].[21] But does this speak to the honour of Racine? Has the latter not fulfilled the theatre's functions of surveillance all too well? Dramaturge of himself, Antoine Vitez would say (and he detested Corneille while he admirably performed Racine).

Between the two, in any case, we can discern – or indiscern – that which theatre, in the throes of the real, can produce in terms of truth. Between the two, to be precise. It is always right, in school, to compare them. And if we no longer do so, it is because truth no longer matters, at least in its theatrical guise. The truth of the link between love, desire, power, and politics is at the point where Racine and Corneille are indiscernible: tragedy, classical. Theatre as superior art.

XXXIX

This number in my rhapsody is of capital importance: here I propose a practical measure, not so much a reform (I have two reforms with enormous consequences up my sleeve, see below) as much as a conservative or preservative measure. A 'do not touch!' that is all the more intensely felt insofar as what is at stake has already been affected a lot.

Everything I have just said indeed comes down to a plea for *maintaining the intermission.* Yes, I beg the theatre and stage directors to maintain or restore the intermissions, no matter how mundane, annoying, or discomforting they may well be. For the state of theatre, which consists in showing and saving, in the form of the State, the state of affairs in the actuality of its future anterior, it is indispensable that the public shows and

21. *Translator's Note*: Here, in the original French, Badiou is playing on the homonymy between *ingénu* ('ingenuous' or 'wide-eyed') and *in-jeu-nu* (literally, 'un-bare-play').

preserves itself as public. The spectators must vanish into a thick and tangible crowd. We must hear the inane commentaries, the exclamations; there must be intrigues, whispers, beautiful women and men compelled to enter into civic competition with the luminous actors. This futility alone gives theatre, this paradoxical State, this contorted form of surveillance of the real, its dark brilliance. To suppress the intermissions is a barbarous, though tempting, act, one that at first sight might even seem salubrious. In sum, and to conclude, to suppress the intermission [*entr'acte*] is a cinematographic act [*acte*].

XL

THE EMPIRICIST: Your intermission will be the place of hatred, since you hold that people hate theatre.

ME: Alas! It is true that the discourse of the intermission is full of reservations, chronicles, absenteeism. If only they would allow the lady with the turban or the svelte gentleman to have a go at it, they would have done such a *better job*! However, these effusions are as indispensable as the bunghole of a barrel.

THE EMPIRICIST: Give me a bit of psychology, just to see. We empiricists like only the objective facts and the mental facts. The list of successes for the season, that's good. But I would have to know a bit more about that hatred of theatre and what it reveals about the ego, you get the gist. You said that the hatred of theatre is self-hatred?

ME: When one hates theatre, one hates precisely this hatred in oneself that consists in shrinking cowardly from the demands of the theatre. The detailed study of the prose of critics always brings out this symptom; that is, that the showy detestation of a theatrical spectacle automatically gets amplified because, really, if the critic had to admit that 'that' was theatre, then he would be all the more discredited in his own eyes for not having been able to give his consent at the time. There is something terrible, even irremissible, about this, which is absolutely proper to the theatre. Nothing can ever make up for, or excuse, not having been a Spectator. Since a representation is an event, those who do not muster within themselves, for the exact moment of its duration, the resources to implicate themselves in that from which a truth proceeds, are for all intents and purposes in the same position as the one who remains quiet in his room while below his window a revolution or a resistance is playing itself out. We understand that they are brought to the point of exasperation and become beholden to the sirens who whisper to them that all that was merely rowdiness and barbarism. That is the only thing that can explain that the most luminous and dense spectacles, those that are the nearest to our real time and tend the most to elucidate our history, are generally declared sinister or catastrophic, or else they are purely and simply passed over in silence. Most often we can expect that some well-intentioned epigones, careful to sidestep the hatred, turn into 'theatre' the grain of truth delivered by the provocation of Theatre, so as to give the retrospective recognition that is owed to what they fled from, in the shelter against art that is culture.

In the open hatred of the theatre I decipher a great and obscure remorse, that of discovering oneself *incapable of* Theatre, and just good enough for 'theatre'. And who would be so arrogant as to believe himself protected from such incapacity and such remorse?

However, we should also consider, with Spinoza, that 'remorse is not a virtue'. To love theatre, by contrast, is a virtue, one that is quite difficult to conquer and nearly impossible to sustain.

XLI

The hatred of the theatre is aimed at those rare representations that mark an event for thought. One does not hate the theatre *texts*. One ignores them (which is another passion). School tended to force the choice: Racine, Corneille, Molière. As a result there remains something *obligatory* that is even more damaging to the free reading of the pieces themselves. Editors do not want any of them, writers do not live off them, readers do not get excited by them.

Consider this singular word: 'piece', like a piece of cloth. It indicates that theatre transcends its texts, which are only pieces, more or less accounted for.

Besides, how do we recognize that a text is a theatre piece? By the fact that it is made of replies? Entire novels are written in this way, and even (Martin du Gard's *Jean Barois*) with the list of the protagonists. Conversely, certain unquestionable pieces are only *one* monologue – this is often the case with Beckett, or Jean Vauthier (*The Fighting Character*). Consider also that certain texts made up of pure dialogue are 'too long', according to general opinion, to be considered true theatre texts. Thus, what are we to say of the original version of *The Satin Slipper*,[22] of which there exists another, very different version 'for the stage'? But who is going to fix the canonical length of a theatre text? The feeling is that certain texts, though written 'theatrically', are not for this reason *of* the theatre.

---

22. *Translator's Note*: *The Satin Slipper* (*Le Soulier de Satin*, 1925), a sprawling work of epic proportions by Paul Claudel, is often considered his masterpiece.

XLII

In fact, the ignorance, or the denial, or the disdain for theatre texts, for edited pieces, has its roots in an essential uncertainty. Can we give a simple answer to the question 'What is a theatre text?' No, because taken in isolation the text does not decide this question: it is only one of the many constitutive elements of theatre.

Only that which has been, is, or will be *played* counts as theatre properly speaking. The event (the representation) retroactively qualifies the text whose written existence nonetheless anticipated it. A text *will be* part of theatre if it *has been* played. Hence: the theatre text exists only in the future anterior. Its quality is in suspense.

XLIII

Here we find again our stubborn analogy with politics. A text of political *thinking* participates in a procedure, it is the inscription of what Sylvain Lazarus calls a 'thinking in interiority'.[23] The true political text is immanent to a 'doing' the way matter is to meaning. The simplest case is that of the directive, whose destiny as thought lies entirely in the action it inspires. Thus the political procedure, which is a practical thought, characterizes the text in which it is stated, as project, as command, as orientation, as political *line*.

Is a written play not much more of a *theatrical line* than a theatrical process? And in the same way that, as long as a play is not performed, we ignore whether

23. *Translator's Note*: See Sylvain Lazarus, *Anthropologie du nom* (Paris: Seuil, 1996); and for a discussion, Badiou, 'Politics as Thought: The Work of Sylvain Lazarus', in *Metapolitics*, pp. 26–57.

its text is truly a theatre text, so too a 'political' text that is subtracted from all practical effects and foreign to all organization will be mere commentary, or philosophy; perhaps it will be written *with an eye toward* politics, but it will not be characterized politically as a political text.

XLIV

The structure of the theatre text, like that of the political text, is that of the not-all. For only that which ex-sists, and that which exists, namely, the representation, or the action, characterizes it qua text.

We can also say this as follows: there is no theatre *book* (if the book is the basis on which a text guarantees itself as the whole to which it belongs), whereas there are certainly books of prose, or of poetry.

There are also no political books. Only texts.

Thus we obtain the inverse of our initial problem: it is not the existence of theatre texts that is the enigma but the fact that there can *only* be texts, and hence something that is of the order of the not-all, the incomplete, the suspended. Fragments *for* the aleatory event of theatre.

What happens is that the real of the representation *takes hold* of the text, and gives it being qua theatre, which it was hitherto only by virtue of its incompleteness.

Every theatre text is thus latent to itself. It lies in the uncompleted nature of its meaning. Every representation resurrects it and brings it to completion.

XLV

But if a text belongs to the theatre because it is a text, and is thus given over to the evental completion of the representation, any book can see theatre take hold of it, provided it first *undoes* it, detotalizes it, punctuates it. Indeed this is what we find: *Crime and Punishment*, as well as *Tomb for 500,000 Soldiers*[24] can be *turned into pieces*. The theatrical action will thus ruin the whole whose glorious redoing it will then ensure.

And inversely, some texts written with an eye toward theatre, because they are too complete, too saturated, too novelistic, will tip over to the side of the book.

Thus there must be a certain intrinsic imperfection to the theatre text, a porosity, a plasticity. Something *simple*, too simple to articulate the whole of a world. Evidence of Molière's universal force *also* lies in the unfathomable equivocity of the characters and the situations, their simplified incompletion.

Indeed, the representation must be able to be something more, just as the application of a political directive must be able to be creative.

XLVI

If theatre is of the order of the not-all, it is essentially feminine. We owe this algebra to Lacan: in the distribution of the sexes, which is less an affair of biological objectivity than of positions with regard to language and of modes in which a subject is linked to it, what counts is the function of the universal, of the 'for all', in the sense in which we say in logic 'for all x, there is the property P', which is written, as everyone now learns on the school benches, $(x)\ P(x)$.

Man is defined precisely by the 'for all', the property being the one inferred from the access to the phallus. 'Man' is whoever sustains the 'for all' of this access,

24. *Translator's Note*: *Tomb for 500,000 Soldiers* is a novel by the French writer Pierre Guyotat (Paris: Gallimard, 1967).

whoever 'totalizes' the property. 'Woman' is whoever opens a breach in this totality, by giving existence to a point, one point at least, such that property is untotalizable: the existential point about which we can say that it is not 'of the all' and which at once makes the whole exist by its exception. It is in this sense that woman is 'not-all' – which already made Hegel say that she was 'the irony of the community'.

If the theatre text is such that only the exception of a representation gives it existence, if qua theatre text it is subject, for its properly theatrical totalization, to the singular point of the instant of the play that itself is outside of the text being played, then we can legitimately say that theatre writes itself 'not-all', as opposed to the compact and self-sufficient world that is the imaginary of the classical novel. It follows that the theatre, perpetually subject to the spectacular vanishing of its being, belongs in effect to the feminine sphere. It, too, is the irony of community. We know, moreover, that by way of transvestism, through sexual insecurity, by the farcical auctioning up of the phallus, theatre posts this latent derision of the glorious 'All' of masculinity. This clarifies why the churches have a tendency to put actors, theatre, and women in the same obscure bag.

But let's complete the dialectic: since theatre is essentially feminine, it is no less essentially a men's affair. For a long time, we know, only men had the right to play theatre, and a hasty examination of the repertoire shows that the writers of theatre are almost exclusively men. There would be this law: men occupy themselves with what touches *too closely* upon femininity, since that is where their desire lies.

A contrario, since the seventeenth century women excel in the novel, which is the exact opposite of theatre, for its compulsion is to set up a whole world according to the completion of writing. Masculinity of the novel, which proposes its completeness to admiration, the Whole of what it stirs up. The novel is a women's affair.

Freudianism affirms all this in three words: 'Girl is phallus'.

XLVII

Grappling with incompleteness, martyred by the not-all, jealous of the novel, the theatre author often wants to *complete* things. Anxious of being suspended from the aleatory character of an event, he jumps ahead of the game in despair. Whence the stage directions, which became almost endless in the nineteenth century, claiming to define the decor, the costumes, the gestures, the figures.... In actual fact, this meant an invasion of theatre by the novel, under the law of an author who would much rather make a whole out of his theatrical proposition.

The theatrical real does away with all that, it expels the novel, and it chastises the stage directions. In this sense, it comes back *to the text*, by freeing itself from the harmful book to which the stage directions had pinned it.

The impossibility of unmooring the text from its novelistic saturation interferes with the representation. We can see this with Samuel Beckett. Roger Blin's productions, which had the author's approval, performed a considerable portion of the stage directions. No matter how great these productions may have been, however, today we should be able to do *something else* on the stage with these unquestionable masterpieces. Patrice Chéreau has tried to do so with Genet, our other great theatre author from after the war (before the war, there is only one, Claudel). However, although the attempt had to be made, this was not a decisive success. What would be needed is a *second intersection* of the text with a principle of completeness (to be brief: with a stage director). Beckett cannot do this, nor does he want to. We understand him, we respect him, but his theatre, which is huge, for the time being lies dormant.

Should we go so far as to make the following atrocious statement: that the death of the genius frees up the incompleteness of his plays? Yes, the theatre is cruel, even if it is not, if ever it is, a 'theatre of cruelty'. It is cruel because it cannot belong to any one person alone.

XLVIII

Paradox: we can thus write for theatre as much in the absolute haste of its urgency (the writer-comedians Shakespeare or Molière) as in the utmost indifference to representation (the early work of Claudel), because the decision will be made retroactively. The *distance* of a text to the theatre varies from zero to infinity, but that is not what decides whether a text is, artistically, a theatre text.

XLIX

I begin a play. I will always end up writing: So and so: '…'. I do not have to describe So and so. He is what he says. Just as only the representation characterizes the text, so too, from within this text, only the proffering characterizes the character. The theatre text is thus the most absolute rule of the word imaginable. 'Words, words, words …' The theatre text exhibits the very law of desire, since here the subject exists only as linked to his discourse. And nothing else.

Except that in the end some body is put forth to be

marked by these words. The actor's is a borrowed body, a precarious body, but also, therefore, a glorious body. 'He *is* the character', says the critic. He is nothing at all, because the character does not exist. He is a body eaten by the words of the text.

Besides, the political text does not describe any actor either. And yet, political action exists *only* in its actors. If I nevertheless describe them, it is no longer a question of a political text but of a history book.

L

The theatre text *is* a text exposed to politics, by necessity. Indeed, from the *Oresteia* to *The Screens,* it articulates propositions that become completely clear only from the point of view of politics. For the theatre text always subordinates its incompletion to the open gap of *conflict.* A theatre text begins when two 'characters' *do not agree.* Theatre inscribes discord.

Now, there are only two major discords: that of politics and that of the sexes, whose scene is love.

Only two subjects, therefore, for the theatre text: love and politics.

Theatre turns these two subjects into one. Everything depends on the knot of this one. And the whole point of theatre today is that neither love nor politics is a force that our time is ready, truly ready, to *clarify.*

LI

THE EMPIRICIST: It seemed to me that, in passing, you were proposing yet another list. Would you mind confirming this, so that I may take note of it on my empirical tablets?

ME: Damn! What list?

THE EMPIRICIST: That of the great authors of theatre, in the French language, and in the twentieth century. I heard: Claudel, Genet, Beckett.

ME: I consider excellent Vinaver, Vauthier, Kalisky, Koltès, and several others.

THE EMPIRICIST: Don't play tricks. Your minimal-list, as you say, the sure names, the contemporary classics that are already guaranteed?

ME: OK, those three.

THE EMPIRICIST: And in Germany, for the same period?

ME: I see only Brecht.

THE EMPIRICIST: Botho Strauss, what do you have to say about him?

ME: If Botho Strauss counts for German, then Jean Anouilh for French.

THE EMPIRICIST: And in Italy?

ME: Pirandello.

THE EMPIRICIST: And in Austria? Peter Handke and Thomas Bernhard?

ME: If Peter Handke and Thomas Bernhard, then Giraudoux and Montherlant.

THE EMPIRICIST: Remind me again of your minimalist one?

ME: Claudel, Pirandello, Brecht, Beckett, Genet.

THE EMPIRICIST: Would you have a list of the great actresses, the great actors?

ME: First a dissertation, in the form of a confession.

THE EMPIRICIST: I knew it!

LII

I want to confess a rather troubling and indefensible thing: I don't love actors very much. I *admire* a few of them, but there is a huge difference between admiration and love. In order for an actor, in his subjective being, to stop provoking in me a feeling of doubt and unease, I must have the assurance that he is also, as if at a distance from himself, the intellectual of his art; I must sense, as the flip side of his agility, the latent solidity of the concept. Someone like a Vilar, when I read him, or a Vitez, when I watch him, are actors, in my eyes, only on the firm basis of some reason. But what is the discernible reason of the actor? In the bygone era of syndicated authority, people tried to present the actor to us as a most ordinary 'worker' who cares for his professional training and his bonuses, who faces the hard realities of the cost of life, and who is on the whole interchangeable, as far as the union's central offices go, with a bank employee. François Regnault has written about the aberration of this image. Closer to the real of the actor is excommunication: everyone senses very well, and I first of all by the limited appreciation I have of them, that actors, even outside the heat of the moment on stage, are the bearers of an irremediable singularity; that they could not function within the ordinariness of the social bond but participate in a procedure of exception; that their job is not one; that their identity does not belong on a card; that their beauty is subtracted from the simple graces of nature; that their voice is something other than speech; and that their gestures come from elsewhere than from the child's apprenticeships.

The actor poses a question. The sheer fact that this false employment exists causes an intellectual principle to teeter. But which principle?

LIII

The ordinary doctrine on this point is well known: having to give figure to all sorts of subjects, the actor would be the actor of himself, an evasive identity, an imitation without any stable point of reference. He would incarnate mimesis itself, and thus, deprived of a ground, or rather having only surface as ground, he would necessarily be someone in whom we cannot have much faith. Someone with not a lot of faith, the church thought. Having an organic need for a ground [*fond*] and a foundation [*fondement*], the church feels threatened in its fundament [*fond*], which is also its (commercial) fund [*fonds*], by the malleability of the actor who can be transported onto all surfaces and who bears witness, by the transports that this transport provokes in the public, to the fact that there exists such enjoyment in imitation that it is no longer even necessary to give it the support of a fixed point. However, the actor outside of the stage imitates nothing, being imitation itself. So it is he, even more so than the theatre, who is suspicious. Like women, about whom for a long time there was a dispute over whether or not they had a soul, the actor could very well show a *subject without substance*. There is a *cogito* of the actor, which is much closer no doubt to that of Lacan than to that of Descartes: I am not where one thinks that I am, being there where I think that one thinks that the Other is.

LIV

Is what teeters then the principle of identity? The fact that One is an Other-than-One? God subverted by mimetic profanation? It is true that regarding this *intimate* question about actors, we must also consider the point of view of the church.

The church, I mean the Catholic Church, is so evidently theatrical in its pomp, the decor that we would try in vain to improve, the purple hangings, the central actor in his white and gold costume flanked by fair-haired sidekicks marked with rouge, the thunderous music or the insidious birdsongs flowing from the organ pipes, tragic or subjugated choruses, a public brought to its knees by the central scene, called the Last Supper, the language elevated toward the esoteric, the unforgettable drama of Presence, the succession marked by turning points, the 'original noise', yes, this same church that every week gathers the entire crowd to its spectacle, that has written and performed for centuries without end the same play – a 'hit', that one, that can only make today's impresario feel crushed – that has invented the Displacement (when the officiant turns around and casts the injunction of the sacred gaze onto the public), the Decentering (when he rises in person on the secret and insurpassable spiraling staircase in order to hurl abuse at the dumbfounded audience), the immobile Pause (when he mutters with his back toward the public, which waits for this suspension of the Acts to end), the cutaway Gesture (when he lifts the wafer box), the Change of costume, the Accessories, and even the Sweetness of the perfumes: Why has this church denounced and excommunicated theatre, thrown the actors overnight into common graves, and found luxury and oblivion in the public's zeal for the theatre spectacle, but not in its own? Is it a matter of jealousy between tour operators, a sordid desire for monopoly? Would it be necessary for all theatres without exception to announce on their billboards only the Mass? For the actors only to be priests, the extras, church boys, the costume designers, embroideresses of chasubles, the musicians, organ players? Would the right to discuss in the great halls the merit of the stars have to be limited, in the eyes of these atemporal and cantankerous authors, to the comparison between Bossuet and Bourdaloue?[25]

25. *Translator's Note*: Jacques-Bénigne Bossuet (1627–1704) was a French bishop and theologian famous for his sermons. Louis

LV

Today we can return to this irritating question with calm: the play of the mass is performed only convivially with the decor of prestressed concrete surrounding a white wooden family table on which an ironmonger's ciborium is placed with negligence. The central actor, who is concerned with differentiating himself as little as possible from his meagre audience, sports a gray jacket; the sidekicks have disappeared; people sit in circles for the sermon, which is reasonable enough since nobody is preached to anymore. Today, in the eyes of the Lord, who is only a Supreme Buddy anyway, who does not have solid excuses to invoke for every canonical sin? Besides, there are no more sins, only drives and fantasies, which an open democratic debate attributes to the legitimate diversities of the ego. And since all of this is done with guitar strumming in the background, nothing distinguishes a church anymore, except for the clock tower, which we expect to be shorter and shorter (because erecting it is offensive), and a cultural and youth centre where we know that any theatricalization, if it ever occurs, comes at the expense of the theatre.

LVI

We will say that the fundamentalists, with their pack of old colonial sergeants, notables from Mayenne,[26] young vindictive bourgeoises and skinheads from the Front National, seek to maintain – aside from Latin and the capital sins – a few effects of the Last Supper, in the ecclesiastical lair that they have actively occupied.

Bourdaloue (1632–1704) was a famous Jesuit preacher.

26. *Translator's Note*: Mayenne is an administrative area of the Loire.

These sinister parodies will not put us off the track; nor will the use of broken harpsichords and patched-up violas da gamba convince us that a baroque musician whose total oblivion honours the taste of the centuries is more vivacious than Haydn. The Mass is worn out, the theatre of Presence is obliterated. At the end of the road we ask ourselves why it considered itself the enemy of all profane theatre, and what this prosecution entailed in terms of truth, even without knowing it, about the profound dialectic of the scene and the soul.

LVII

Rather than the vacillation of a principle of identity, what intrigues me in this malediction is the fact that one can, and must, suppose some thought as regards to women. The church for a long time has had doubts whether they had a soul. Now, I hold that theatre is tied to this very obscure problem in a crucial way: the soul of women, whether it exists.

It is not for nothing that for so long, and in so many places, only men exerted the function of actors. Contrary to the banal hypothesis, which claims that people want to keep the maternal substance of women away from the perils of imitation (because about a woman actor, it must be said, one cannot put one's trust in what she reproduces), I think that insofar as women are held to be imitators by nature, they would have corrupted the enjoyment of imitation that men had to acquire. Men take imitation to extremes, because they have to imitate it. Men imitate imitation, and that alone makes the actor, and thus theatre. Besides, we can say that an actor, and it matters little in this regard whether it's a man or a woman, is first of all the one who *imitates a woman*, because it is the one who *imitates imitation*.

Everyone knows that a man playing the woman makes for theatre, which is not in and of itself the case of a woman who plays the man. As for a woman who plays the woman, that is an ordinary occupation in life, as long as she does not go so far as to play this play itself, and thus to imitate the imitation that she lavishes as woman. It is certain that actors subvert the difference of the sexes, and I am sure that what unpleasantly vacillates in me when I come into contact with them is this very difference, of which I am a strong partisan. But this subversion involves the twists of imitation to the second degree, it does not present itself in equivocation. I do not believe at all in the theme of the androgynous actor; to the contrary, there is nothing more distinct in theatre than men and women. Actors and actresses present the difference, they consolidate it, but this is also in order for imitation to circulate in such a way that this given is on the one hand emphasized and on the other decentred and turned back upon itself. A major stake of theatre, already suspect to every church, consists in proposing the following thesis: the two sexes differ radically, *but* there is nothing substantial in this difference. Theatre introduces us, through its play, to this first point of ethics: know that no difference is natural, beginning with the difference that institutes that there are men and women. We can say this differently: *if* women have no soul, then nobody has one.

LVIII

Theatre carries with it from the origin an essential 'feminism' that is based not on equality but on the substantial nothingness of that which marks the difference of the sexes, the purely *logical* and transparent character of this marking. Or again, if you want, *the* woman does not exist, since a man or a woman, actor or actress, is justified in producing its signs or its in-sign-ia. This alone can explain the fact that theatre among the Greeks presents powerful figures of women, in a society in which women are politically absent, socially confined, and philosophically kept in a barbarous background.

LIX

I seem to observe, contrary to a widely held opinion, that there are fewer great theatre actresses than actors. It is certainly more difficult for a woman to be an actress, insofar as it belongs to the essence of theatre to imitate the feminine imitation. An actress functions to the third power (imitation of the imitation of the imitation), her play is necessarily mediated, on at least one point, by the masculine arrangement. She must *also* become one of those men who alone had the right in ancient times to be an actor; she must, on stage, reconquer at all times this right, which no institution can guarantee. It is indispensable not to lose sight of the fact that an actress, a woman, plays what a man would consider necessary to play a woman who plays a man. This requires extreme poise of hysteria itself. The actor can always keep steady on the margins of equivocation, he *finds a foothold* in the limits of his own universality. An actress is always at the limits of the absence of limits, she functions *on the edges of the void.* Many actresses have tried to fill this void with the return to simple imitation, which is emphatic, subjugated, tearful. The ethics of play imposes upon actresses an unconscious distance that for them is the pinnacle of mastered artifice, the pinnacle of art. Whence also the fascinating grip exerted by a great actress, more generic than an actor, closer to humanity, which is this very void on the edges of which she holds steady.

LX

THE EMPIRICIST: Come on! You could take a few risks! Names! Who are those fascinating and ever so rare actresses? And who are those emphatic, subjugated, tearful ones?

ME: Their glory is so assured that I can cite, without harm to them, two actresses whom I don't like at all: Jeanne Moreau and Maria Casarès.

THE EMPIRICIST: You are not mincing words here! And those you like?

ME: Given my principles, they cannot be actresses in the sense of a proper name or a supposed subjective substance. They can only be actresses *in the evental singularity of a spectacle.*

THE EMPIRICIST: No false excuses. The list!

ME: Every empiricist is a British police officer. Good. In one breath:

- Madeleine Renaud in *Happy Days* (Beckett/Blin)
- Claire Wauthion in *Britannicus* (Racine/Vitez)
- Madeleine Marion in *Bérénice* (Racine/Vitez)
- Maria de Medeiros in *Death of Pompeius* (Corneille/B. Jaques)
- Edith Clever in *The Oresteia* (Aeschylus/Stein)
- Jutta Lampe in *Phèdre* (Racine/Stein)
- Nada Strancar in the Molière cycle (Vitez)
- Dominique Reymond in *Falsch* (Kalisky/Vitez)
- Maddalena Crippa in *The Triumph of Love* (Marivaux/Vitez)

I am at the end of my roll call, but there are others.

THE EMPIRICIST: It's an eccentric list. I'll let you go back to your sexual dogmatizations.

LXI

In general, bad theatre, capable of reassuring the church, is theatre that naturalizes differences. It gives up on the ethics of play insofar as it distributes substances. It pretends that the imitation of the imitation was only the redoubling of imitation, which supposes *that there is something to imitate*. Now, the second imitation, which alone presents differences as objectless transparencies, is the imitative procedure, which does not exist except in the act itself. It is the play itself, the play of play. It *must* surprise, unless it pretends that there exists a nature behind the role. Taken by the debates over whether Hamlet is a phobic or a schizophrenic, or whether he does not know how to come to terms with castration, Lacan puts an end to all this with the remark, which has always made me very happy, that Hamlet *doesn't exist*. What presents itself is the actor, and if his performance presumes the existence of anything like Hamlet, theatre is dissolved. Bad theatre, which from the start I have called 'theatre', turns the actor into the stabilized professional of a network of vocal signs and gestures by which we recognize that something exists. He stirs up a complicity of recognition. He avoids the spectator, the attentive work of thought that, starting from incalculable scenic presences, consists in gaining access to the universal conventions of difference without an object. 'Theatre' proposes to us a sign-ification of supposed substances, and Theatre, a procedure exhibiting generic humanity, that is to say, indiscernible differences that *take place* on stage for the first time. This is why there is something painful in the attention that is required from the spectator of Theatre, whereas ease and easiness are the rule in 'theatre'.

LXII

Here is what I would propose: bad theatre, 'theatre', is a descendant of the Mass, with its established and substantial roles, its natural differences, its repetitions, its falsified event. It is where one gets a taste of, where one gobbles up, the virgin, the aging hysteric, the tragic actor with the loud voice, the virtuoso of lamentations, the shivering beloved, the poetic young man, just as one eats, in the guise of the host, God. One comes away from this with one's dispositions taken care of and put on display. One obtains salvation on the cheap. Genuine Theatre turns every representation, every actor's gesture, into a generic vacillation so as to put differences to the test without any supporting base. The spectator must decide whether to expose himself to this void, whether to share in the infinite procedure. He is summoned, not to experience pleasure (which arrives perhaps 'on top of everything', as Aristotle says) but to think.

LXIII

A capital consequence of all this is that the central virtue of the actor is not technical but ethical. One must always stay at a distance, just short of the quest for an effect, because every effect presumes that the imitation is straightforward, that it has an object at its disposal. One must hold steady at the edges of the void, at the edges of the abyss, against which it is always reassuring to invoke precisely the power of effects. One must at all times be *singular*. Singularity is much harder than originality, for a mere original ends up playing itself, becoming the nature that supports the differences. Singularity is a composition without a concept. The result is that there is no 'good actor', if by this we mean a 'guaranteed' actor, no matter what the circumstances on the stage are. This guarantee can only be technical. It is only in the stage event, when the ethical virtuality of play is achieved, that an actor or an actress can excel. But the stage event in turn demands the conjunction of two artists: the theatre writer and the stage director. An actor or actress is, in the end, *the ethical in-between of two artistic propositions*.

LXIV

Finally, what the church abhors in theatre and especially in the play is the fact that to the natural ethics whose spectacle it organizes, theatre opposes an ethics of the event and of singularity. For the church, art is ornamental; with its power, it heightens the scenic repetition of the figures of the sacred order. For true theatre, art is initial (the poet's text) and terminal (the representation governed by the stage director). Between the two, there is no order to mediate, not even that of the profession, technique, or talent. There is an ethical availability that is directed against all substantialism, against all fixed conceptions of the roles, the people, or the representations. The actor exhibits onstage the evaporation of every stable essence. The decisiveness of the bodily and vocal gestures in which he or she presents himself or herself serves above all to establish, in delight and surprise, that nothing coincides with itself. The ethics of play is that of an *escape*, we could say: the narrow escape [*l'échappée belle*]. In particular, the actor operates against every natural theory of difference, and specifically of sexual difference. His or her play makes an artifice out of what we believe to be the most evidently *given*, it combines that which we imagine to be forever separate, it separates that which seemed an acquired unity. The actor's play is always *between-two*. This between-the-two *operates* in the pure present of the spectacle, and the public, who in the Mass is molded by Presence, gains access to this present only in the aftermath of a thought. What true theatre presents is not represented, and the word 'representation' is misplaced. A theatrical spectacle is every evening an inauguration of meaning. When the text and the staging know how to solicit the virtual ethics of play, the actor or actress is the pure *courage* of this inauguration.

LXV

A second crucial paragraph, this LXV! And, thus, LXVI as well! Here I propose a reform, a real one. A radical reform: that of the greeting, relative to the way in which, at the end of the play, the public *joins* the actor lined up by the clapping of the hands.

Like any reform, especially one announced as radical, mine stems from an axiom made dubious by obnoxious reasonings. The axiom, which I uphold under any circumstances (but that is the least of things for an axiom), is that of paragraph LXIII: the actor is not an artist, but a moral hero. He or she depends not on the critique of judgement but on the critique of practical reason. The actor's ethical proposition presupposes an artistic proposition, and even two: at the source, there is the proposition of the theatre author, or the poet; at the other end, there is that of the artist of theatre, or the stage director. The only histrionics belong to the author and to the stage director. The actor is the interstitial seriousness of this double histrionics.

From this axiom it follows, by the simple use of a few laws of logic, that it is not only useless but also noxious, even blasphemous, for actors and actresses to come and greet the public at the end of the spectacle. The eventual introduction of the empirical and almost prurient appeal to applause and shouted bravos into the austere execution of the actor's duty inevitably corrupts its very substance. If they are booed, it is even worse, because either it is the saintliness of the moral Law itself, to which they are publicly sacrificed, that is thus covered in jibes, which would be horrifying enough; or else it is the actors who, having failed (being bad actors), are blamed for *not having* held up the moral order of the Subject, which is nefarious because, precisely, a supposed failure of the imperative of Play can be referred only to the inner judgement of the actors and actresses, and not to the sanction of some public disapproval. In order not to expose the actor to the temptation of a reward nor the public to the philistinism of blame, the most effective measure is to omit without delay the miserable habit of gathering before us, with all kinds of hypocritical faces, the actors immediately after they have achieved that alone which counts, namely, their Act, the everyday and collective redemption of the sexuated Subject.

LXVI

Will there then be no more salutation at all? No! Because the same reasoning that excludes from such clowning the noble soul of the actors, devoted to ethics, also necessarily summons those who by contrast are devoted to art, that is, to some generic truth. If the duty of the actors consists in subtracting themselves from praise as much as from blame, the duty of the authors and stage directors (and of their acolytes: decorators, musicians, costume designers, light technicians, ...) evidently consists in begging for them, or to be more precise: it consists in inquiring into the collective disposition of the spectacle. The author and the director of a spectacle will thus be *forced* to come and greet the public every evening. We could easily show that if they are raised up to the clouds by a delirious public, it is perhaps an excellent sign as to the positive values of the inquiry into the spectacle's genericity. If they are abundantly booed, it goes in the direction of negative values, unless we have to conclude the opposite, based on the hypothesis of the public's cognitive rut. Still, we will always be able to come to a conclusion and thus contribute to the becoming of some artistic truth.

What to do if the author is dead (we will posit that a dead director is no longer capable of directing)? As with any imperative, the one relative to the salute by the artists cannot allow any exception. Therefore, every evening an actor will be summoned to represent the dead author and to endure in his or her stead the bravos and the boos. The objection does not hold that in this way it is an actor who salutes, contrary to the fatal consequences of the axiom, for the actor in question does not salute, he plays the author who comes and salutes. And the actor invests all his ethical conscience in this performance, deaf to the rumour in the auditorium, which he knows is not addressed to him but to the dead author for whom he is a placeholder.

Of course, it is excluded that the actor returns *afterward* to greet the public in his own name, with the aim of receiving compensation or punishment for his performance, executed according to those well-known roles of the repertoire, 'Dead Molière greeting the public after *The Misanthrope*', 'Dead Shakespeare booed after a calamitous *Hamlet*', and so forth. Once again let us leave it up to the actor's conscience alone to know whether the respect of the Law was guided by his obsequious gestures as an author in an inquiring salute, or if he for a moment imagined that people were clapping for him, the actor, in the vain nostalgia for those corrupt times when the public was exposed, as in a fair, to morality's immortal monsters.

LXVII

But the spectator: in the name of what, under what pretext, would he remain in his seat, if not because on behalf of the State, in which theatre participates, you are obliged to remain seated where the usher puts you, just as you are obliged to remain in your seat in school? Besides, it is always a bit in secret that, in entire rows contaminated by darkness, on the loud tip of their toes, or after the first intermission, those who refuse to listen any more leave, or flee. Usually they are all the more numerous, as a rule, the more the spectacle is innovative and dense, unless they are held back by the fact that the cultural opinion press (that is, when all is said and done, *Le Nouvel Observateur* and *Libération*, but these two organs, in matters of theatre, do not possess the most assured taste, nor do they have the capacity to distinguish between the conceptual summons and the razzle-dazzle that flatters our neuroses) has covered the spectacle from which our spectator is about to flee in all the perfumes of what the chitchat among teachers will have to be about.

We can already distinguish two regimes of the fixity of the gaze: the pedagogical constraint and snobbism. Theatre as dismal pedagogy (an aspect of Brechtianism, if not of Brecht himself), and theatre as the basis for cultural glossing, as the serious index of collective chatter. Thus ....

LXVIII

THE EMPIRICIST: Of this 'razzle-dazzle' for the 'flattering of neuroses' with which the honourable opinion papers would like to pull the wool over our eyes, could you not cite a few titles to me? So that I may no longer be lost ...?

ME: The best example is not from theatre but from dance: Pina Bausch, that inadmissible darling.

THE EMPIRICIST: Leave dance alone, please, since you have no clue about it. A paradigmatic example of snobbish spectacle, in theatre, and a recent one, for the spectator shamefully fooled by the press, that's what is needed.

ME: I didn't say that the press fooled the petty-bourgeois spectator, since it is also the latter who fools the press, because the press concentrates his predisposition to flee the theatre by keeping him there *for all the wrong reasons.*

THE EMPIRICIST: An example.

ME: Books of theatre, except those by the theatre artists Stanislavski, Meyerhold, Brecht, Jouvet, Vilar, Vitez, or those, all too rare, by spectators armed with a destiny for theatre, such as Regnault, are made up only of images and examples. They are old as soon as they appear in print, because theatre is measured in terms of eternity, not by staying on but by disappearing. The eternal essence of a spectacle lies in its having-taken-place, which no scattered journalistic account can restitute. All the more so since, if I mention a spectacle that in my eyes is mediocre but glorious in the opinion of these papers, weak in Idea but strong in Doxa, nobody will know, six months or one year from now, what I was talking about.

THE EMPIRICIST: Do you think I am going to applaud this pompous feint? You quoted *Libération* and *Le*

Nouvel Observateur, which should suffice to guarantee that you will not be understood by any eternity! If you do not give me my example, I will have to think that you are pusillanimous.

ME: With arguments like these.... OK, let's say *Zerline's Tale,* text by Broch, directed by Grüber, main role Jeanne Moreau. I insist, first of all, on underlining my admiration for Broch's *Death of Virgil* and, second, that Grüber is in my eyes one of the five most important European directors working today. But *Zerline's Tale* is a spectacle that is both weak and low, aesthetically and ethically demagogical. My thesis is that Grüber, aware of this, has slept, completely drunk, throughout the rehearsals, on the bed that appears in the back of the stage set.

THE EMPIRICIST: You will be hard put to prove such a thesis.

ME: So what? As Rousseau said: 'Let's put aside all the facts.'

THE EMPIRICIST: One fact that you will not put aside is the list of the five greatest theatre directors in Europe.

ME: You have a good ear.

THE EMPIRICIST: So?

ME: Chéreau, Grüber, Stein, Strehler, Vitez.

THE EMPIRICIST: You're not exactly 'making space for the young'!

ME: For some years now theatre has not been doing very well.

THE EMPIRICIST: You make me laugh! It never goes well with theatre.

ME: It's true that, because it started one day, it cannot perish.[27] Then again, I am only one spectator, I do not see everything, I do not even see a reasonable not-all.

---

27. *Translator's Note*: Badiou is parodying and inverting Hegel's famous dictum according to which everything that is born one day deserves to perish.

I have a very poor knowledge of Russian directors. Peter Brook is also not too far from the top. There is a particular problem with Bob Wilson, who is not really a 'theatre director' but rather an 'author of representations', one whose spatiotemporal imageries oscillate between the upsetting and the repugnant (in the sense in which I am repulsed by having to endure what is shown and sounded there, as in a kind of puerile and artificial Nature). And so many others, which we would have to examine *case by case.*

LXIX

After all, is what I call the razzle-dazzle of neuroses so far removed from what Aristotle calls catharsis? Whether the passions are large or small, it would always fall to theatre to purge us from them (or to purify them? That's the whole problem). And is what I describe as a pedagogical constraint not the effect of distancing or alienation? Brecht's non-Aristotelian theatre, which must inscribe us in the dialectical circuit of class consciousness? We would thus still be at the same point:

- *Either* theatre is a capturing machine of desiring identifications, and its thrust is by analogy psychoanalytical – it transfers, displaces, filters and purifies that which the sexual underside of the speaking being attaches to it in terms of latent meanings;
- *Or* theatre is a perfected pedagogical apparatus, and its thrust is by analogy philosophical – it distances the Idea in the veil of representation, and forces us to an elucidation that, if we did not have the mirage of voices and bodies to elicit it, we would not even be able to know for sure it exists.

In neither case is there a direct mention of the classical rule ('the point is to please'). The spectator would be there, not for pleasure, but for a therapy or an apprenticeship. This would explain why, in spite of its so-called popular or trivial variants as well as its bourgeois degradations, theatre remains invariably *serious*.

LXX

So: in a location tied to the State, and conditioned by an ethics of play, a spectator-subject would be put in place by the seven constitutive elements of theatre in such a way that this subject either transfers onto the simulacra of the stage whatever insists in his or her desire, or else he or she occupies, with regard to the Idea latent in the golden and scarlet appearances, the universal position of the philosopher without knowing it.

LXXI

At once the unfathomable mystery of the theatre (but, in the end, what is theatre?) would occupy the material position of another question, which we know to be clarified only very little: that of the relations between psychoanalysis and philosophy. Theatre would be the *effectiveness* of this question, summoning the spectator to decide (if he or she is on the point of the real of his or her desire, it is psychoanalysis; if he or she is instructed by the path of the Idea, it is philosophy), without there ever being a way of knowing how to decide, because if one interrogates the spectator upon exiting, he or she will only be able to say 'it was good' or 'it wasn't great', aphorisms from which neither the psychoanalyst nor the philosopher would be able to draw the rule of their triumph.

LXXII

So Theatre would be the following: a complex machinery (seven elements), creating a situation whose *objective* dialectic is sustained by the majesty of the State, whose *subjective* dialectic engages an ethics, especially with respect to the difference between the sexes, and whose *absolute* dialectic brings into being a subject-result, a spectator, about whom one cannot decide whether the whole operation assigns him to the real of his desire or to the power of an Idea.

LXXIII

Of this notion that theatre has always been the materiality of an undecidable problem between philosophical mastery and the therapeutics of desire, we can no doubt find confirmation in certain hesitations on the part of Aristotle. However, it is even clearer in that which opposes, say, Plato to Lacan (but also to Freud) as soon as it is a matter of examining the theatrical poem. The former is alarmed by the fact that the poem may claim to educate the young in the one area in which the philosopher would much rather lord over them, namely, regarding what is meant by knowledge of the truth, how one can know the humans and the Gods. In his endless and painful polemic against theatre and poetry, Plato confronts a *rival* and banishes him from the place where the philosopher has seized power. By contrast, it is evidently an *accomplice* whom Freud and Lacan interrogate when they turn to Sophocles or Shakespeare.

Rivalry and complicity have this in common: they both presuppose the communality of some stake. Who does not know the fact that an accomplice is a potential rival, precisely because of that which, between the two, counts as one, and only one, for example, the crown? See, for instance, the lessons of Shakespeare, precisely on this topic: *Macbeth,* and so forth. We can thus be sure that philosophy and psychoanalysis recognize that the operations of the theatre take place on their respective terrains, and thus *at the intersection, which is always in dispute, of these territories.* Psychoanalysis, which sees here a social and artistic extension of its field, is glad to acknowledge this and takes its concepts (Oedipus) and its cases (Hamlet) from the repertoire. Philosophy is more reticent due to the fact that, for philosophy, the Idea latent in theatre can lay claim only to the generic particularity of art, and not to the master's Great Lesson.

But perhaps it is above all the case that philosophy sees in theatre, which always fascinates it and gets it all worked up, a mode of the Idea that is *infected, always, by desire.*

Theatre would be: philosophy seized by debauchery, the Idea on the auction block of sex, the intelligible dressed up in costume at the fair. Thus, on the side of philosophy (the Idea, the intelligible), it would rival with the master, and on the side of debauchery (sex, the street fair), it would be the accomplice of psychoanalysis.

Theatre: the putting-into-bodies of the Idea. From the point of desire, it is its life; from the point of the Idea, it is its tomb. Whence the anathema and the disputes. Theatre as bastard philosophy, or philosophical bastardy: principled impurity, diverted lesson, all-too-serious analysis, all-too-ludic truth to be assured. A revolving door.

LXXIV

A brief look back. I have distinguished the objective theatrical dialectic (the State of theatre), its subjective dialectic (the ethics of play), and its absolute dialectic (the putting into place either of a desire or of an Idea).

There are *roles* that correspond to these instances of the dialectics of theatre. The *stage director* is the regent of objectivity, he or she signs the spectacle, and besides he or she is also often the 'boss' of the theatre in question. The actor, as we saw, is the body of subjectivity. And the spectator occupies the position of Absolute Knowledge.

There are also *financial relations* to these instances, because in the world as we know it every dialectic traces its outline against the background of the general equivalent of money. The financial point of the stage director is the Subsidy (objective, static), that of the actor is the Expenditure (subjective, sumptuous), and that of the spectator is the Revenue (insufficient, as is always the case of the Absolute).

LXXV

I am still not satisfied. Let's see, what *truly* happens when I am a spectator? 'An example!' the Empiricist would say, who has been mute ever since I gave in to the concept too much. What happens when I attend a representation of *Bérénice* directed by Vitez, or by Grüber?

But first of all, what happens when I read *Bérénice*?

LXXVI

When I read *Bérénice,* the principal effect is that of Eternity. There is something diamond-like. This is unlike the novel, which carries with it, sticking to its sole, a whole range of detailed stories, decors, and trajectories. The great text of theatre, because it is open and incomplete, because it will be played through the ages and by human beings who are indifferent to the whole context of this text, human beings who have changed gods, whose city no longer has the same form, and whose loves no longer have the same law, this text must possess the powerful simplicity of the atemporal, it must bespeak a *generic* humanity, capable of passing from actor to actor, from body to body, from State to State, all the while preserving its fundamental meaning. *Bérénice:* love, the State, renunciation. Conjunction and disjunction. The glacial transfixing clarity of language, this music stopped in the tracks of its constant precision, all this formal work is only the receptacle of the Simple, the ingenious capture of an essence that bodies, voices, and breaths will incarnate for centuries.

Bérénice, Titus, Hamlet, Orestes, Mesa, Estragon, Scapin, Alceste, Peer Gynt, Rodrigue are proper names of genericity, they belong to a subject-language that is spoken by nobody in person, being the eternal flip side of any historical language. Men and women designated by these names *can exist at any moment.* The text merely is the guarantee, the depository, of this virtual existence, which nothing can interrupt except the blaze of libraries.

This is not at all like Swann, or Goriot, or Saint-Preux, or Don Quixote. About these great archetypes from the novel, we will say that *they exist forever in the text,* and not that they may exist at any moment. The characters of the novel are *immortal,* those of theatre alone are *eternal*: where a dialectical time is elaborated that subtracts itself from time (who fails to know that a spectacle retains time?), I may *encounter* them, since they have become *out-of-time,* but capable of becoming temporal before our very eyes.

There is thus – first strand in the knot of theatre – an eternity latent in the text and in that which singularizes it among other texts: the genius of its simplicity, its genericity, the fact that any proper name here is *also* a common name and that, based solely upon the duration of the text, we can have, forever, the race to pass on the torch of interpretations.

LXXVII

And now when I watch *Bérénice*? There is the ineffable moment of each representation, that which I will never be able to retain or describe, this false time within the suspension of the true, this immense history that is told to me with the speed of lightning.

Vitez will tell me, with his own diction projected far beyond a body shrunk by gesture, the pain without concept of the intellectual Antiochus, unable to retain a woman either by the exploits of power or by the violence of desire, and who still and always believes that to tell subtly of his misery may convince her, as if love or desire could be caught in the rhetorics of lack, as if the confession of a defect, no matter how artistic or sincere, could – by looking for the all-merciful Mother – lead to anything other than to missing out on the woman.

Grüber will arrange, in a kind of trembling of the origin, the separation of men and women, at the same time as the legendary History of Empires. Speaking among themselves in a low voice from one side of the stage to another, marking by their gestures, their poses, their fabrics the fact that they are indeed the worn-out Rome, Egypt, Persia, the actors insert Racine in a revised vision of Hegel, in which every scene must be read as a figure of individual consciousness at the same time as it is a figure of historical consciousness. The same void separates the hearts and opposes the dead kingdoms.

But all this is in the moment, under the visible and artificially unified constraint of the seven constitutive elements of theatre. There are only displacements, lights, breaths, voices. There is also myself, captive in my seat, and thinking only of seeing and listening *exactly*, which in and of itself constitutes an effort more akin to the understanding of a mathematical statement than to the beatific enjoyment in which television images leave me basking. Precisely in theatre *there are no images*, there are only sensible combinations whose perception, if it is sustained with exactitude, *clarifies the moment*. Titus' manner (because *it is* Titus, it is not an image of Titus, nor imitating Titus, who is inimitable, being only the eternity latent in the text) of wobbling, or of vanishing at all times (Grüber) or, on the contrary, his manner of falling asleep, satisfied and cunning, so as to avoid the stories and the reproaches (Vitez), organize in the moment the *encounter* of Titus and the spectator that I am. We had a date, now is the moment. Whether he vanishes into the shadows of Empire or falls asleep amid the duplicity of intrigues, it is he whom I have encountered, at two different moments of his eternity.

We will therefore say the following: representation makes an encounter, in the moment, of that which the text holds in the eternal. That is to say, a *good* representation does so (a *bad* one is a missed encounter: there is neither eternity nor the moment, there is only the painful duration of the spectacle). This encounter functions for the spectator as an elucidation of the present. Or again: because one encounters in it that which a proper name (Titus) designates in its eternity, the instant of theatre can be understood after the fact as an *instant of thought*. Theatre would be the perception of the instant as an instant of thought.

LXXVIII

There is reading, there is seeing, but there is also that which *operates*, that which remains. Of this encounter of the eternal in the elucidation of the instant, what is the effect on the spectator who endures it? Catharsis? Moral, intellectual, political education?

I am reminded of a comment from Vitez: that the real function of theatre consists in *orienting us in time*, in telling us *where* we are in history.

Theatre as a machine for answering the question 'where?', a localizing machine, a machine for a topological relation to time.

Grüber, by means of an instantaneous encounter with Titus the eternal, would tell me that today we are at the pinnacle of the original discord between men and women, precisely because they are represented as equal, or even as identical. And he would also tell me that History is finished, that it has always found itself in the guise of its finishing, that our world, which is so prosperous, is above all and everywhere *tired*.

And Vitez, by means of an instantaneous encounter with the same Titus, seized at a different instant of his eternity, or with his companion Antiochus, would tell me that the critical intellectual, who wanted to remain in the proximity of the powers or the parties that be, has lost his energy and his reference points, that as a result, confusion rules over matters of both desire and politics, and that to the great question 'What is it whose death this century is experiencing?' we must answer, with the same outburst that Vitez the actor lends to Antiochus when the play comes to a close: 'Alas, communism!'

LXXIX

There thus would be three terms, and not just two:

1. the eternity of the figures, held in reserve by the text, which amounts to a simple capacity to exist at any moment
2. the moment of the representation, which artistically puts in motion the machinery of an encounter with the eternal, and which thus proceeds to a perceptive elucidation of the instant as an instant of thought
3. time, in which the elucidation of the instant serves to orient us, with this instant introducing a 'cut' in time, in the obscure thickness in which we are situated

Theatre would possess such complex and aleatory ingredients only because it ties together eternity, the instant, and time. And its destination would be:

- the elucidation of the instant by an encounter with the eternal
- the orientation in time by the after effect of this encounter

We are all the more capable of orienting ourselves in time, the more we have experienced the instant as thought (should we say: just as the instant of insurrection sheds a lasting light on our tasks in our time? And is this not its only function? But in this analogy what is it that would represent the eternal? What is *historically* eternal? Perhaps, precisely, politics *itself*? Such as it happens in its text?).

LXXX

This experience, this localized fiction of an image of politics that combines, in the effort of becoming a spectator, the instant, time, and eternity, is so fundamental to us, and so precious, that it is inadmissible for it to be reserved for a small number.

The 'problem' of the theatre public (its disappearance, or almost, its scantiness, its identity...) has primarily been phrased in terms of class analysis: it was a question, by way of lower prices and alliances with the syndicates, to bring the excluded from the *banlieues* or 'poor neighbourhoods' into the theatre. Or else it was necessary to go and 'perform' in the towns and villages. This was the era of popular theatre, of culture for all, of theatre as universality above and beyond class. This required austere theatres, reinforced concrete, the visibility of machines, the repudiation of all velvet and gold, the destruction of the boxes where the noble ladies planted their décolletages. We have lost the velvet and the gold and the décolletages, without having seen the real crowds come in with their blue collars and their berets, even less the totality of the actual modern proletariat, those profound intellectuals with their unimaginably complex factory lives that are our Moroccans, our Algerians, our Senegalese and our Malians, our Turks, our Yugoslavs, our Pakistanis, and so forth. Distributive equality has not established its rule over the theatre halls.

And then, after the brief pause of militant street theatre, the theatre of soapboxes and of agit-prop, sketched out in the wake of May '68, there came capitulation pure and simple. Theatre found stability as a 'middle class' activity, surrounded by bourgeois 'theatre' and by 'theatre' for television, both of which are connected in a consensual backwater of sorts, in which an unchanging cast of the same few actors stumbles through a few equally unchanging flabby stories.

LXXXI

Of course, we could argue that theatre will gather some real crowds only when there will have been a real of the crowds, politically educated. Theatre is, I will allow myself this word whose wear and tear is without cure, the very type of communist fiction. As a temporal elucidation, it could serve as an intimate analyzer of whatever meaning the crowd holds and as a projection of the conflict that constitutes it. Under the fainting lights, it could be the difficult flickering up of a public state of affairs, and better yet: the potentially controversial distribution of matters both public and private.

But what is to be done in the meantime?

LXXXII

Here I propose my second reform, which is so wide-ranging that it is a pleasure to see. It can be summed up as follows: *our presence in the theatre halls must become obligatory.*

LXXXIII

In order to realize this important reform of public morals, we must find support in our national traditions of Jacobinism. I have sufficiently demonstrated the necessary link between theatre and the State for this support to lose all its apparent arbitrariness.

We would obviously begin with the Comédie-Française, which is a royal institution that defies time. It would first of all be charged with establishing an affiliate in every Prefecture, a departmental French Theatre, endowed with adequate resources, a permanent cast, an administrator appointed by the political power, and so forth.

Aside from its activity in the Great Theatre of the Prefecture (vast and luxurious, offering *to all* the golds and velvets of tradition), each departmental theatre would be responsible for organizing, in the towns of some importance (let's say, starting at 3,000 inhabitants), at least four representations per year, three plays from the repertoire and one new creation.

It is understood that special buses – the service of theatrical gathering – would crisscross through the neighbouring villages so as to bring their population into town when the departmental theatre is in season.

LXXXIV

Once such logistics were put into place, what would be the forms and means of the theatrical obligation?

Every resident aged seven and up, except in cases of force majeure, would be expected to attend at least four representations per year.

Theatre would obviously be free. It is true that, aside from its evident secular nature, popular theatre in the fifties already wished to be free. However, in Jules Ferry's[28] model the essential element was forgotten: the obligation.

Control at the entrance would be limited to putting

28. *Translator's Note*: Jules Ferry, French politician, established free education in 1881, the so-called Jules Ferry Law.

the official stamp in the theatre card that every resident receives at the start of each year.

The compensations and the punishments must always be of the essence: the theatre card will be joined to the tax declaration. Spectators who are particularly zealous, whose card offers a constellation of stamps, would be entitled to substantial deductions. By contrast, the recalcitrant ones, those who fall short of their legal theatre obligations, would pay a painful fine of a fixed amount, whose profits would go entirely to the theatre budget.

LXXXV

Such an abundance of theatre presupposes a real effervescence of the creative effort. The State would organize every year a major public competition for the writing of theatre plays. An international jury composed of ten noted directors would select at least twenty plays, which would be performed the following year throughout the national territory. The public success of these plays, as witnessed not by attendance (always maximal, given the obligation) but by the studied sentiment of the spectators, the critics, and so forth, would decide their inclusion in the repertoire.

Should we distinguish, as was previously the case with the entry exam for the Conservatory, between a competition for comedy and another for tragedy? This question of the *genres* of theatre is at the same time crucial and obscure.

LXXXVI

In comedy, everything attached to eternity, as has been said for some time now, depends on the phallus, that is to say, on that which supports that there can be signification at all. The instant of comical theatre is made up of the showing of the phallus, of eternity turned into the farce of a somersault offering a glimpse into its tiny glory.

The latent eternity of the text of comedy sketches a repertoire of functions, a fixed symbolic treasure from times immemorial: the old fogy of the Father, the Lover, the Parasite, the Vixen, the swanky Soldier, the Pedant, the Miser, and so forth: the whole 'there is' of generic social signification. The instant pins this onto the stage. The effect of temporal orientation results from the fact that the functions and occupations enter into a rapport with what we might call a diagonal character, who is less a function than the zero point in which all functions are reflected as such. It is a question of the subtle slave, of the treacherous servant, charged with *dissolving* before our eyes the fixed connection of meanings, by means of an infinite social knowledge.

A modern comedy should tell us where we are in terms of what is socially serious and in terms of its dissolution.

Unfortunately, the social is taboo in our regimes of power. It has become categorically statelike, the object of innumerable *guarantees*. But you cannot have an inoffensive comedy, I mean: a comedy that would not offend anybody. How can we arrange onstage, with the necessary violence, the Syndicalist, the Parliamentarian, the Priest, the Doctor, the Journalist, but also Mittérrand, John Paul II, or Deng Xiao Ping? Comedy is something other than cabaret. It tells of the other side of signification, it inflicts wounds for which there is no cure. Today, the tiniest Aristophanes would be dragged into court for defamation, and the play would be prohibited in a summary judgement, to be enforced immediately. There can be no comedy, in the classical sense, where corporations and private owners hold the right over their public image.

It is furthermore doubtful whether our societies present the recourses necessary to support the dissolving diagonal. In an unpublished play, *Ahmed the Subtle*,[29] I had recourse to the figure of the Arab worker to occupy this place of the diagonal. But this is only a hypothesis.

What is clear is that for the moment there exists no modern comedy (this does not mean that there exists no funny play, which is another question altogether).

LXXXVII

In tragedy, eternity is that of being, and not that of the phallus. However, being is indifferent to meanings. Whatever eternity there is in the tragic comes from non-sense, the name of which is: Fate. The latter's instant onstage can only be death. If this mortal instant teaches us something about time, it is because it establishes a rapport between the will (against the backdrop of the will-to-die) and the non-sense that undoes it. The tragic play represents the subject not against the complicitous and laughable background of meanings (comedy) but against the neutral backdrop of being.

Tragedy speaks to us of: Being and Time, *Sein und Zeit*.[30] It asks of us to think where we stand, in historical time, with respect to being. We could also say that it demands that we take a stand with respect to the history of truth.

It is a sign of comedy that it produces laughter, but the production of tears is not a sign of tragedy. Fear

29. *Translator's Note*: This play has since been published: *Ahmed le subtil: Farce en trois actes* (Arles: Actes Sud, 1994).

30. *Translator's Note*: Badiou is referring to the title of Martin Heidegger's work, *Sein und Zeit* (*Being and Time*, 1927).

and pity? Rather anxiety and courage: anxiety over the excess of being over all meaning, and courage in nevertheless inscribing at least one truth.

The tragic hero is always the one who chooses truth rather than meaning. Death in this whole affair is only a figure of theatre, the aesthetic side of the operation. Death is this figural commodity that turns the choice between meaning and truth, onstage, into an elucidation of the moment.

Is it possible to have a modern tragedy? More easily no doubt than a modern comedy. The obstacle is the 'democratic' consensus, the consensus of right. There can be no tragedy in the moderationism of right. Tragedy can tell of the origin of a law (Aeschylus, *The Oresteia*) or of its fall (several tragedies by Shakespeare), but it cannot inscribe itself in its celebration. Already the Greek tragedies, in the regime of the agora, appealed to the ancient monarchs. I have relied on this point to establish the collusion between theatre and the State, but we can also use it to discern that which in tragedy is so harshly nonconsensual.

A modern tragedy would have to summon us inevitably to think through the nonsense of law. In the moment of death (but who today is capable of dying onstage?), it would say that 'democracy' is the opposite of truths. Or rather, it would indicate to us, against the backdrop of nonsense and in a paroxysmal state of the history of truths, *another sense* of 'democracy', one compatible with the event of something true, a sense that precisely would not be the trickling down of meaning, and that would not mistake as a form of thought what is only the depressing conflict of opinions and interests.

For the moment, there exists no modern tragedy.

LXXXVIII

Neither tragic nor comic, contemporary theatre is oriented toward simple *declarations*. This is the status of Beckett's fables, haunted as they are by the monologue. Declarations bearing upon what there is (not a whole lot, but not nothing either), upon what there is not (neither comedy nor tragedy), and upon what there could be (first of all, no doubt, a modern tragedy). Contemporary theatre desires the tragic, without for the moment disposing of the means necessary for it. It has the desire to offend meanings, it desires the comic, but it does not have the means for it either. It is between-the-two, desired tragedy, measured comedy.

But that it could be otherwise does not depend on it. Its time will come, together with ours – uncalculable, but as a bonus on top of hard work, of restricted action. Which is where *a few* truths lie in the balance of meaning.

LXXXIX

Theatre is the proof, for any real and present state, of the link between being and truth. This proof is valid even when theatre shows signs of faintness on this or that point, which is the case of our current situation.

To conclude, let's listen to this perfect definition of the theatrical act, which comes to us from Mallarmé: 'This was to take place in the combinations of the Infinite face to face with the Absolute. Necessary – the extracted Idea. Profitable madness. There one of the acts of the universe was just committed. Nothing else, the breath remained, the end of word and gesture united – blow out the candle of being, by which all has been. Proof.'

Mallarmé adds: 'Think on that.' In effect: think.

NOTES, REFERENCES, REGRETS[31]

For this small book [*Rhapsodie pour le théâtre*] I have freely used previously published texts, particularly from the journal *L'Art du théâtre.*

This journal, edited by Antoine Vitez with the enthusiastic support of Georges Banu, published ten issues between 1985 and 1989, after which it was suspended. It was the result of a joint edition between the National Theatre of Chaillot (from the time of Vitez) and Actes Sud.

Thanks are due to this journal that, by its sheer existence and its link to the essential contributions of the Chaillot theatre between 1980 and 1988, fostered my taste for writing, as a spectator and as a playwright, about the strangeness of theatre.

The few notes that follow are numbered with reference to the paragraphs in the main text.

6. The texts in Stéphane Mallarmé's *Divagations,* and not only the subsection titled *Scribbled at the Theatre,* contain an intricate and dense meditation on the theatre, one of the most profound I can think of, situated between the theory of writing (or of the Book) and the theory of society. For Mallarmé, theatre simultaneously touches upon the mystery of letters and the mystery of the collectivity, or of the Crowd. The poem, in its essential vocation, thus confronts theatre as the only *public* fiction that, from the beginning, rivals it.

Let us recall that *Afternoon of a Faun* was first written for the stage and that *Herodias* was supposed to be what I call (in paragraph eighty-seven) a modern tragedy. This

31. The translator's interpolations herein are shown in square brackets.

tragedy did not take place, nor did the Book of which it was supposed to be an integral part.

28. The Cultural Revolution, about which countless and outrageous stupidities are told today (which is only normal at a time when the market economy presents itself as the supreme collective and ethical value), led to intense debates about the meaning of theatre. Hundreds of texts, both passionate and brutal, as all revolutionary texts are, appeared on the subject between 1965 and 1976. Since nobody reads them or even knows of their existence anymore, let us cite a few of them:

– *Procès-verbal des causeries sur le travail littéraire et artistique dans les forces armées, dont la convocation a été confiée par le Camarade Lin Piao à la Camarade Kiang Tsing* (a pamphlet containing texts from 1964 to 1967) (Paris: Éditions en Langues Étrangères, 1968).

– *A propos de la révolution dans l'Opéra de Pékin* (Paris: Éditions en Langues Étrangères, 1968).

– *A propos du 'système' de Stanislavski* (*Hongqi* nos. 6–7, 1969).

[In English, see 'Summary of the Forum on the Work in Literature and Art in the Armed Forces with which Comrade Lin Piao Entrusted Comrade Chiang Ching', in *The Chinese Cultural Revolution*, edited by K. H. Fan (New York: Grove Press, 1968). For a commentary, see Jean Esmein, 'Cultural Politics', in *The Chinese Cultural Revolution* (London: Andre Deutsch Ltd., 1973).]

30. Personal plug: the complete text of *L'Écharpe rouge* appeared in 1979 with Maspero editions (which has since then become La Découverte).

33. I probably did not mention Irish theatre as much as I should have. Sean O'Casey's plays remain among the rare examples of theatre whose precise historical articulation (the national and social struggle of the Irish) does not block universality. And John Millington Synge's *The Playboy of the Western World* is a marvelous play.

I still remember a lyrical and solid representation of it, directed at the time by Brigitte Jaques.

I would also like to mention that Stanislawa Przybyszewska's play *The Danton Affair* has been translated into French [by Daniel Beauvois] and published by Éditions L'Âge d'homme (Paris, 1983).

41. Jean-Louis Barrault and then Antoine Vitez finally brought the complete text of *The Satin Slipper* to the stage. In this way they demonstrated that it was indeed a theatre text. About the event marked by Vitez's production, the reader can consult François Regnault's *Le Théâtre et la mer* [in the same collection as the French edition of Badiou's *Rhapsodie pour le théâtre*] (Paris: Imprimerie Nationale, 1989). Here one can find, among many other precious things, a slightly different reflection from mine about the link between theatre and the State and about the present conjuncture of this link.

43. Regarding the concepts of politics as Sylvain Lazarus rethinks them, the reader should consult the following three short texts (all of them included in the series 'Les Conférences du Perroquet', Éditions Potemkine):

- *Peut-on penser la politique en intériorité?* (no. 4, November 1985)
- *La catégorie de révolution dans la Révolution française* (no. 15, 1988)
- *Lénine et le temps* (no. 18, March 1989)

[Lazarus's conception of politics is given a systematic form in *L'Anthropologie du nom* (Paris: Seuil, 1996).]

46. The formulas of sexuation according to Lacan can be found in particular in *Seminar* 20, *Encore,* chap. VII (Paris: Seuil, 1975). [In English: *Feminine Sexuality,* trans. Jacqueline Rose (London: Macmillan, 1982).]

51. Regret. I really like Aimé Césaire's plays a lot, too. In Peter Handke's theatre, there are parts that deeply touch me and that bear no resemblance to anything

else. I am thinking of the worker's monologue ('Rubber! Rubber!') in *Walk About the Villages*. The overall form and the preaching are the most shocking to me. And, when all is said and done, what should we think of Federico García Lorca? Djuna Barnes's play *The Antiphon* (translated by Natacha Michel with L'Arche editions) is a stunning piece of writing. Not negligible either is Eugene O'Neill's invention of the whole tradition of American melodrama, an almost nauseating mix of family matters and psychoanalysis catapulted on the audience. There are also the Irish, as I mentioned above. Is it honest to hide, under the pretext that it has been such a long time since we went to see them, that in my youth certain plays by Ionesco (*The Chairs*) or Sartre (*The Devil and the Good Lord*) left a deep impression on me? And so on and so forth. From time to time, however, one must redo one's personal Pantheon, even if it is with a suspicious eagerness that one throws the once honorable bones out onto the streets.

59. The function of the transvestite, which is so important in theatre, with its detours and its difficulties, sheds some light on the dialectic of the actress. On this topic, see Judith Balso's remarks about Vitez's version of *The Triumph of Love* by Marivaux (in the newsletter *Le Perroquet* [no. 29, May 1991]).

60. Regret. I would nevertheless want to add in extremis the incredible performance by Dominique Valadié in the monologue of the Moon (*The Satin Slipper,* Claudel/Vitez).

78. The idea of theatre as an operator of historical orientation has been developed by Vitez in a conference (unpublished) for the series of Le Perroquet.

86. Personal plug: The play *Ahmed the Subtle* was read by Vitez at Chaillot in 1988. I swear under oath that the audience was cracking up.

87. It is striking to note that Beckett's characters never

die. Therein lies the (bitter) observation of a contemporary impossibility to present 'dying' on the stage, or even behind the scenes.

89. Mallarmé's phrase comes from the preparatory notes for the unfinished text *Igitur.* [English translation by Mary Ann Caws available online at *http://www.studiocleo.com/librarie/mallarme/prose.html*]

2

THEATRE AND PHILOSOPHY

To have chosen 'a short philosophical treatise' as the subtitle for my 'Rhapsody for the Theatre' presupposes that, cutting diagonally across many centuries, there exists a singular relation between the artifices of the spectacle and the severity of philosophical argumentation.

Indeed, the least one can say is that philosophy and theatre, as a general rule, have kept only very distant relations, even dreadful ones.

From the origin, Plato objects to the theatre because of its use of role play, masks, and imitation. Theatre would be suspiciously polymorphous, vacillating in its relation to semblance. Theatre distances us from the solar stability of the Idea; it showcases the sharing and the inverting of appearances, instead of the tenacity with which the philosopher seeks to climb up toward the principle of what is. Besides, the being of 'what is' is scarcely a category in theatre, which rather privileges the scintillating passage of becoming, the sexual confusions, or the treacherous paradoxes of fate. And the worst is that this constant imitation seizes upon the spectator-subject with a degree of violence that one thought was reserved for the powerful revelation of truth.

Rousseau, in his fulminating *Letter to d'Alembert*, is severely critical of the theatre, this time from a moral and civic point of view. The spectacle means representation, whereas the essence of legitimate political power, of democracy, is the presentation of the people as general will. Theatre corrupts the presentation with representation. It captures the public from the bias of the untransmissible, even unavowable obscurity of its desires. To this, one will oppose the civic festivity, which is the innocent presentation of the people to the people, in a gathering sufficient all onto itself, showing nothing but the immanence of the will.

Perhaps the most unique example is that of Nietzsche. From this fierce anti-Platonist one would have expected a revision of the negative verdict concerning the theatre. But the opposite is the case: the hatred of theatricality lies at the heart of Nietzsche's aesthetics. From *The Birth of Tragedy* onward, after having shown that music (and not theatre) constitutes the Dionysian essence of Greek art, Nietzsche denounces Euripides for the Socratic and theatrical corruption of great art. In his final diatribes against Wagner, the principal accusation is that the latter has prostituted music in favour of the theatrical effect. Theatre is a false thinking, a plebeian simulacrum. For the thinking will, it substitutes a vague promise that is capable of sustaining only a hysterical sense of the stage. Theatre, qua thought before thinking, is a spiritual demagoguery, which is opposed to the power of life. It is the nihilist art form par excellence. The direct art form, the art that affirms life and 'gives a new name to the earth', is dance. Zarathustra has 'the feet of a mad dancer', but he hates the theatre. Let us say that theatre is opposed to dance, it is the ruin of dance.

Let us remark that if philosophy proposes various classifications of the fine arts, it is rather rare for theatre to be explicitly included in these meditations, and even rarer for it to occupy a preeminent place in the hierarchy. For Hegel as well as for Deleuze, sculpture is dominant; music is for Schopenhauer; the poem for Heidegger; painting for Merleau-Ponty. Theatre as such (I mean: the theatrical representation) is the ugly duckling, if it is not the excluded, banished, vulgar character in this assembly of the Muses.

There are important philosophical projects today that concern poetry (Lacoue-Labarthe, Nancy), painting (Lyotard), cinema (Deleuze)... but nothing on theatre. It is true that the American philosopher Stanley Cavell takes his critique of the philosophies of knowledge all the way into the vicinity of Shakespearean tragedy by showing how skepticism is the true theme of *Othello*. But this reading concerns the text, or the tragic poem, and it eludes the performative aspect of the representation. Now, theatre qua theatre cannot be reduced to the text, even if it presupposes it.

Besides, what are the modern texts on theatre? They are texts by theatre people, circumstantial texts such as notes, articles, or haphazard observations; texts subject to the urgency of the moment, to repetition, and to didacticism; texts that immediately *accompany* the theatre. Moreover, they are often barely written but rather rewritten or re-transcribed texts, by Stanislavsky, Meyerhold, Jouvet, Brecht, Vitez, Strehler.... Even François Regnault, who certainly is not lacking in matters pertaining to philosophy, writes on theatre from behind the curtains of actual theatre halls.

And even then: Strehler does not hesitate to declare that actors are not artists; that he himself, as stage director, is not an artist; that the only artist is the author, the poet; and that the point is to be at his or her service. But if theatre is merely at the service of the poem, it is not an art form in the full sense.

Everything thus seems to argue for an essential delinking between philosophy and theatre, and even for a kind of artistic inconsistency of theatre itself.

And yet, the crossings between theatre and philosophy are also obvious, and like the patent delinking between the two they hearken back to the origins. The theatricality of Plato's dialogues is undeniable, and it is not for nothing that the *Symposium* or the *Alcibiades* are frequently put on stage. No matter how much he rails against the theatre, Nietzsche nonetheless roots his thought in the meditation on that of Aeschylus. Karl Moor, the hero of Schiller's *The Robbers*, is not for nothing one of the great figures of the becoming Absolute of self-consciousness according to Hegel. Rousseau wants no theatre in Geneva, but he writes an operetta, *The Village Soothsayer*, and works hard for its success. Classical philosophy seeks to present itself in the form of dialogues, as in the case of Malebranche who serves up a reply to himself – in the role of the 'Christian philosopher' – by an unlikely 'Chinese philosopher'. The romantics follow in the footsteps of the classics: Schelling, too, writes certain philosophizing scenes, which allow him to give voice to a woman (if not, where is the sexuation of discourse in philosophy?). Sartre finds in theatre the esoteric form that suits his doctrine of freedom. In Brecht's didactic conversations, the question master is called 'philosopher'. Moreover, Brecht's constant aim was to found a 'society of friends of the dialectic'. Today, philosophers are frequently invited to the theatres. I myself go there, and I write theatre plays, all the while trying hard to think through the strange surprise of the play of performance.

In this way we are led to believe that the link between

theatre and philosophy is tense, paradoxical, and probably as decisive as it is obscure.

In order to bring some clarity to the matter, we must start from the categories through which philosophy seizes upon art in general, and upon theatre in particular. 'Philosophy', here, will be taken to mean that discourse in which the central concept, whatever its unique name may be, is ultimately that of truth.

I believe that we can then discern three canonical figures in the philosophical seizure of art: didactic, romantic, and classical.

Didactic: its thesis is that truth is always external to art, that the register of art is that of semblance. Art is therefore suspect, because it passes off as a truth what is only a simulacrum. It is all the more suspect, insofar as its emotional power, the immediate interpellation of the mind by its sensible resource, diverts us from the long and painful detours required by the conquest of the 'true truth.' The function of philosophy, therefore, is to place art under surveillance so that at least its formidable subjective efficacy may be at the service of truths. As regards theatre in particular, the demand will be for it to be the heroic fable of the Idea. Its ambiguity will be chased away. This demand is clearly sensible in the concrete analyses of theatre, whether of the tragic or comic poets by Plato, of Molière or Racine by Rousseau, or of Wagner by Nietzsche. In all these cases, there is an active censorship of ambiguity. The hero of the fable is seized upon in his spectacular, litigious exposure. It will be asked that Alcestis, the possible hero of the intransigent truth, not be mocked the way he is virtually everywhere on the stage; that Socrates be spared from ridicule; that the kind of Christian half-wits like Parsifal not be passed off as heroes.... Philosophy gives us a lesson in theatrical didactics by criticizing and rectifying its equivocations and impostures.

Classical: its thesis is that, while truth is certainly external to art, this externality is innocent. Indeed, for the classical figure, and in this sense classicism begins with Aristotle, theatrical art by no means aims at the truth and, thus, is not a simulacrum or imposture. Its function is not cognitive, but practical: theatre captures the subject in an operation of identification and transference, by which this subject projects and deposits his or her passions. Theatrical art offers a therapeutics, and not a propaedeutics. Insofar as there is imitation, it is only so as to enable the transference. This imitation does not possess the structure of a simulated truth; it obeys the rule of an entirely different category, which is the properly imaginary category of verisimilitude. Consequently, there is nothing to be feared in theatre, since it does not at all rival with philosophy (which is the search for the truth) but accompanies it with the beneficial effects of appeasing its internal tensions and obscurities.

Romantic: its thesis is that art alone is capable of concrete truth. Art is the descent of the infinite Idea into the sensible. This is an involuntary and suffering descent. Such is the whole thematics of romantic drama. *Je suis une force qui va*: 'I am a force to be reckoned with.'[1] This drama of the suffering Idea, of the finite crucifixion of the Infinite, echoing a dialecticized Christianity, exalts theatricality as visible passion, as the exposed flesh of the True. Compared both to the abstraction of the concept and to the pettiness of the real world, theatre is legitimated as visible mediation, as the Passion of the true gathering a people.

Has our twentieth century, with regard to these three figures, invented anything new? I don't think so. The

1. *Translator's Note*: This is a line from Victor Hugo's play *Hernani*. The phrase also serves as the subtitle for the first volume of Max Gallo's biography, *Victor Hugo: Je suis une force qui va!* (Paris: XO Éditions, 2001).

romantic, classical, and didactic ways of seizing theatre have been circulated, some of their presuppositions have seen innovations, but they have not been replaced by a different figure.

For instance, it is totally evident that Marxism has adopted the didactic figure. In the theatre, the official thesis of the 'positive hero' means precisely that ambiguity cannot be kept up to the end, that the spectator must be warned about the subjective place of truth. Even in Brecht's refined Marxism, didacticism is central. For Brecht, there exists an external truth, which is even scientific in nature: dialectical and historical materialism. The stakes of theatre consist in making visible the relationship of subjects to this truth, which the immediate world obliterates. The central question, then, is that of the courage of truth, of mother-courage (or of bitter-courage).[2] Or, also, that of cowardice, or of the oblique nature of the relationship to truth in the labyrinth of circumstances: such is the essential figure of Galileo.

The difficulty of this great and inventive project lies in its constriction by epic form. For the epic is the formal arrangement for the showing of courage. Now, even in order for the spectator just to be able to follow the spectacle, the epic form presupposes a collectively assumed system of values. And we know that this system of values is obsolete today. This is why, after Brecht, who is a great theatre artist, there only has been a fixed or fossilized Brechtianism, which then became impracticable. It is also why today the whole question is how to put Brecht's pieces on stage *in a non-didactic arrangement.*

On the other hand, it is equally evident that psychoanalysis upholds the classical thesis. Here theatre

2. *Translator's Note*: A pun on the homonymy between *la mère-courage* ('mother-courage') and *l'amer courage* ('bitter-courage'). *La Mère Courage* is the French translation of Bertold Brecht's 1939 play *Mutter Courage und ihre Kinder* (*Mother Courage and Her Children*).

is the circulation of the object of desire, the exhibition of family complexes, the exacerbated drama of sexual difference. The spectator finds him or herself *fixed* in an imaginary arrangement in which what shines forth and vanishes is the object that constitutes him or her in his or her desire. Theatre is a kind of short psychoanalytic cure. And conversely, the cure itself is presented as the scene of transference, or, as the analysts like to say, 'another scene'.[3]

The difficulty here is that theatre, thusly conceived, is more illuminating for psychoanalysis than psychoanalysis has been of service for the theatre. In fact, we have especially become privy to a kind of sophisticated psychologization of the art of the playwright, as can be shown in the theatre tradition that most openly assumes this identity, that is, Anglo-American theatre since Eugene O'Neill. Once past the almost mythical, revelatory power of this last playwright, the classical-psychoanalytical thesis leads to the luxury boulevards, of which Harold Pinter is the emblem.

And, certainly, the romantic figure too has been maintained, via German hermeneutics, by what I will call the theatre-poem, characterized by a lyricism that is scarcely distinguishable from an ornate and visible poetic saying. Here the risk is that of an extreme rarification, of an arbitrarily scenic reading, or of a theatricality that is wholly subtracted from the dialectic of play and performance.

Fossilized Brechtianism, psychoanalyzing boulevard theatre, and annulment of the performative aspect under the effects of the body-poem indicate the contemporary

3. *Translator's Note*: *ein andere Schauplatz*, 'an other scene' or 'an other stage' was Freud's name for the place of the unconscious and of dreams. It is borrowed from Gustav T. Fechner. See Sigmund Freud, *The Interpretation of Dreams*, *The Standard Edition of the Complete Psychological Works of Sigmund Freud*, trans. James Strachey (London: Hogarth Press, 1953), vol. 5, pp. 535–6. The expression also became the ground for Lacan's more abstract and abridged expression of the Other.

impasses of the triplet that seizes theatre: didactic, classical, and romantic. Let us say that the twentieth century has saturated the three inherited relations between theatre and philosophy. It has certainly been innovative, but from within a categorial saturation.

The most contemporary target is therefore the possibility of a fourth relation: neither didactic (thus post-Brechtian), nor classical (thus post-Freudian), nor romantic (thus post-Heideggerian). I will name this relation immanentist, by which I mean the following: theatre neither has the truth standing outside of it, nor must it be content with a *catharsis* of the passions, or of the drives, nor finally is it the absolute descended onto the scene's finitude. Theatre produces in itself and by itself a singular and irreducible effect of truth. There is such a thing as a theatre-truth, which has no other place except the scene.

Unable here to lay out the complete conceptual framework for this hypothesis, I will limit myself to four traits, all of which have a purely descriptive character. Besides, these different traits are modulated in the book that I am hereby introducing.[4]

1. Theatre is a *completion* or an *accomplishing*. The theatre text or, if you want, the theatrical poem, is only virtual, or open-ended. It is attested to as a theatre text only by the representation. Theatre properly speaking is the virtuality of the Idea that has *come to arrive* in the perishable actuality of the scene. But also, this properly theatrical virtuality exists only in this coming or arriving. Theatre is the coming that alone accomplishes the Idea. This is what I will call the evental dimension of theatrical truth.

4. *Translator's Note*: Badiou is referring to his treatise *Rhapsodie pour le théâtre* ('Rhapsody for the Theatre'), translated above.

2. Theatre brings about an encounter between eternity and the instant *within an artificial time*. Say: Hamlet, such as he is latent in the Shakespearian text, is an eternal figure. In the theatre, he exists only in the instant. But these instants of the play compose an encounter of sorts with the eternal figure. And this composition is the time proper to the theatre: a time whose artifice alone authorizes the encounter on the stage of the forgotten instant of the play and the eternity of its figures. This is why a successful representation is first and foremost the imposition of a time. I suppose that the art of the stage is before all else the art of the composition of time. Voices and bodies are crucial, but only because they are the *matter* of time, the time that each evening is experimented on the stage, as the joint proposition of instants of play and of the eternity of the figures. This is what I will call the experimental dimension of theatrical truth.
3. Theatre organizes, through its temporal setup, a collective summoning of the Idea. It is an activity that is essentially (and not accidentally) public, which is something, by the way, that the text of a play in itself is not at all. Event (as the efficacy of the virtual) and experience (as the composed artifice of a certain time) are *for* a public. This is what I will call the quasi-political dimension of theatrical truth.
4. Theatre indicates where we stand with regard to historical time, but it does so in a kind of readable amplification that is its own. It clarifies our situation. Antoine Vitez used to insist on this point: theatre clarifies our inextricable existence. I am thinking for instance about Alain Milianti's spectacle based on a text by Jean Genet on Shatila.[5]

5. *Translator's Note*: In September of 1982 Jean Genet went to Beirut together with Leila Shahid, and found himself in the midst of

> This very beautiful theatrical time situated us with regard to the Palestine situation, but according to a measure that went back all the way to the *Iliad*, which we also encountered in the temporal rhythm of the scene. Thus the situation that was being invoked became enlarged, carried toward the timeless, without for this reason being denied, but rather intensified thanks to the constructed play of the instant of an actress and a Greek horizon of figures by which 'Palestine' meant for us both an urgent summoning and the arrival of the eternal ground of our time. This is what I will call the amplifying dimension of theatrical truth.

There you have the singularity of the theatre-truth, seized in a purely immanent way. There, on the stage and nowhere else: a quasi-political experimental event, which amplifies our situation in history.

So then, assuming all this, we can return to the question of the relation of theatre to truth, and thus to philosophy.

A truth (for there is never 'the' truth, there are only multiple truths) is eternal, singular and universal. I ask you to grant me these three features, because the suppression of any one of them abolishes the true, whether in favour of temporal versatility, dogmatic abstraction, or cultural relativism.

---

the Sabra and Shatila massacres. He would write testimonies about his experience, most notably in 'Four Hours in Shatila' as well as in *Un captif amoureux* (*Prisoner of Love*), a mixed-genre book that is part travel narrative, part testimony, and part commentary about his visit to Jordan a decade earlier. In 1991, in Le Havre, Alain Milianti produced a theatre adaptation of Genet's testimonies about the Shatila massacre. See the documentation gathered in the collective volume *Genet à Chatila* (Arles: Actes Sud, 1994). In English, see Jean Genet, 'Four Hours in Shatila,' *Journal of Palestine Studies* 12.3 (Spring 1983), pp. 4–5; and *Prisoner of Love*, trans. Barbara Bray (New York: New York Review of Books, 2003).

Theatre arranges an experimental, precarious and public machinery that:

- presents the eternal in the instant;
- singularizes the relation to this presentation (since the spectacle is always unique, precarious, abolished);
- amplifies its own event in a collective summons, which is in principle universal (since the empirical limit of the public is a matter of indifference, the public representing humanity as such).

Thus, the theatre as truth is a special linkage of eternity, singularity, and the universal, from the triple bias of the poetic figures that it embodies, the fugacious uniqueness of the play, and the universality of the public.

To be more precise, I will say that *theatre makes a truth out of the different possible forms of the collective relation to truths*. Or that it arranges the figures of the contemporary subject who falls prey to the truths of its time.

To the truths, and not to the opinions. Therein lies the force of all genuine theatre. The false theatre, which I call 'theatre', by no means represents an encounter with eternity, since it calls upon vulgar opinions; it has no universality, since it is aimed at an audience that is pre-formed by its opinions, most often of a repulsively reactionary nature. True theatre, the Theatre which Mallarmé declares is a 'superior art', is an encounter organized in an unprecedented and singular time, which in principle is universal, with the eternal figures of the subjectivization of the true.

In this sense theatre is a true art, insofar as it is never (except in the decadent forms of the majority) a phenomenon of opinion. We can see this in two of its characteristic features. The first is the irreducibility of the theatre to all forms of being photogenic. True theatre is invisible to the television camera. A televised play is a journalistic approximation of a representation, and never the transmission of the representation itself. Theatre is absent from it, and all we obtain is vague and obscure information about what happened. Only the theatre of opinion makes the crossover to the screen (tonight's *Masterpiece Theatre*). But everyone knows that all truth and all art have been extirpated from it from the start. Precisely in this 'theatre', there is never *this* precious night in which I encounter an eternal, singular and universal theatre-truth. There is an average and anonymous evening in which nothing has happened to anyone, except sinking into the basest of opinions. The second feature is the extreme difficulty found in theatre criticism. Why? Because criticism gives us the ingredients of theatre, it sums up its materials (the decor, the text, the actors, the ideas for the mise-en-scène…), but it never manages to transmit to us *what has happened*. But this alone is what matters, because a representation, the essence of which is the composition of a time for the encounter, cannot be reduced to its canonical ingredients. In fact, the critic (but can he do otherwise?) functions as a mediator between the (evental, experimental, quasi-political, and amplifying) theatre-truth and the supposed opinion of the reader. The point is to seduce (or reduce) this opinion, by means of easily recognizable categories (a valid piece, good acting, good costumes, emotionally moving…). Unfortunately, between truth and opinion, there is not, there cannot be, any acceptable mediation, since all truth is a hole in opinion, a catastrophe of opinionating. It would be necessary for the critic to suppose on the side of the reader, not opinion but thought, and thus for the critic to become a witness of an artistic event that summons up a singular emotion of this thought. This is a nearly impossible job, I admit, but no more difficult, in any case, than to convince a reader of the intrinsic importance of the proof of a new mathematical theorem.

All this is a negative way of saying that theatre, in the singularity of one evening, operates in the realm of *truth*. Philosophy, therefore, can learn from it so as to grasp what is a precarious, experimental, ephemeral rupture with the regime of opinion. To grasp what is a scenic instant of eternity.

We could say that, understood philosophically, theatre is the vanishing life of a collective contemporaneity of truths. The plurality of the play and the complexity of its composition give figure to this disparate contemporaneity.

What are then the difficulties of theatre, and of the renewed linkage between theatre and philosophy, for all of us?

The first difficulty stems from the fact that our time celebrates opinions, polling them and indulging in them to the point of a cult. The supreme value of our time is not truths, but 'freedom of opinion', which most often means: the 'freedom' to give the same opinions as the rest of the series. Now, theatre must create collective situations in which our time is evaluated by *subtraction from all opinions*. Theatre can only be this place that is rebellious to the cult of opinion, and about which everyone will therefore say that it is not 'democratic'. Let us thus desire a theatre for the thought of everyone, against the opinion of everyone, and in this sense, as Vitez used to say, an elitist, or non-democratic, theatre.

The second difficulty is that our time has no use for eternity. It is on the side of calculation and instantaneity. Next week for it is beyond the reach of meaning. Now, theatre shows that any real measure of time involves a presentation of the atemporal. It exhibits the maximal conjunction, that of the instant and eternity. It constructs its own time, whereas we endure the time of banality. Theatre indicates to us that in order for us to know who we are, where we stand and what our time is worth, we need Hamlet, Antigone, Solness the builder, Bérénice and Galileo, who exist atemporally only in the experimental and singular time of the theatre. Let us therefore desire a theatre that is indifferent to the present time, an ill-timed theatre, an untimely theatre, and a theatre that runs counter to its time.

The third difficulty is that our time shows few signs of courage; it is a time of fear and of the desire to take shelter. Why? Because courage is always the courage of a possibility that one invents and defends. Now, our time has very few possibilities to push for, it continues whatever exists, and is content to persist in growth, or to seek protection in de-growth. Theatre, for its part, is a place that requires what Hölderlin would call the courage of the poet. In it humanity is suspended from its most extreme possibilities, deciding its destiny on the stage, in the most extensive spectrum of surprising possibilities. Let us therefore desire a theatre without parsimony or reserve, a theatre that summons humanity to exceed itself, a theatre that contradicts all existential miserliness, a theatre of insecurity.

The fourth difficulty is that our time is not very prone to writing theatre texts. A theatre text, as I said before, is open-ended and virtual. It must withstand an infinite number of interpretations, and expose the eternity of its figures to countless instants, to a large variety of temporal compositions. This is why great theatre texts are so rare and at the same time so universal. One can play Molière in Baghdad, in Bombay or in Ouagadougou. A text that supports being exposed to such multiform encounters must be endowed with a powerful *simplicity*. Combined with an original and intense poetics, the theatre text has something typical, a force of stylization that is the culmination of virtuosity, a brilliant proximity to generic humanity. Theatre, and theatre alone, enriches humanity with timeless exemplars of its general destiny:

Don Juan, the Miser, Tartuffe, Oedipus, Nero, the Jester, Caliban. As well as with situations that bear no date: the undecidable (Hamlet), the killing of the Father (Orestes), the declaration of love (Marivaux), the splitting of the subject (Pirandello), the decision (Brecht), the departure of a woman (*A Doll's House*), the knots of hatred (Racine), the potential of the forbidden (Claudel), the reasons of the State (Schiller), the miracle (Polyeucte).... Yes, the genius of theatre lies in the clearing of every trait that would be too particular, in the generic resourcefulness of simplicity, which is also the most difficult thing to invent. But our time never stops bragging about its 'complexity'. It is blinded by its own machinery, which it believes to be subtle, whereas it is only mechanical. The 'complexity' of our contemporary world is rather the exterior appearance of the automatism of Capital. It attests to the *incapacity for the simple*, to thought that is prisoner to opinions, the apparent diversity of which is only the mask of impotence. Because our world has in fact the inapparent simplicity of a false multiple, it always finds itself in the realm of thought cluttered up by the useless. Whence an anti-theatrical, pseudo-complex, atypical and vaguely baroque propensity *for nothing*. Let us therefore desire an extreme and simple theatre, which typifies and summarizes our superficial hodgepodge. Let us desire the experiment of radical and eternal texts, such as those of Beckett, Genet, and Guyotat. Let us desire telling to those who dream of dramatic poems: 'Dare to write! Dare to simplify and risk the world! Dare to show types that are eternally exposed to the encounter of an evening that our time, like all those before it, holds in its visible poverty!'

Our difficulties are also, as is the case of any point of the real, the key to our possible desires. Conditioned by an artistic activism of these desires and wills, theatre can be instructive for philosophy, which must itself dare – against the 'complex' idea of an end – its own simple regrounding. Theatre must repeat what is the most precious: to show the Idea in the ordeal of the ephemeral – something which Antoine Vitez called a 'theatre of ideas'; every evening to triumph over its apparent and material defeat; to be worthy of Mallarmé's words: 'The drama ... is resolved immediately, the time to show its defeat, which unfolds in a flash.'[6]

6. *Translator's Note*: A quote from Mallarmé's project for the Book. See sheet 4(A) in the manuscript reproduced in Jacques Scherer, *Le 'Livre' de Mallarmé* (Paris: Gallimard, 1957).

3

THE POLITICAL DESTINY OF THEATRE YESTERDAY AND TODAY

The fact that precariousness belongs to the essence of theatre is something that we rediscover after each representation when, back in the street, the feeling of a bitter dispersion comes over us while we search for words to retain a moment longer what was a feast for thought, an ordeal of conviction, which suddenly threatens to become nothing more than a jarring and lacunary ensemble of painted bodies and excessive voices. Nothing is more difficult to *fixate* than the unsurpassable greatness of theatre, all the more so in that the invariance of the text creates the illusion of being a solid support in which we nonetheless find only the occasion for what, one evening, strikes us in decisive ways. In the theatre, no matter how sturdy, the text is only pre-text, and eternity is given only in the material creation of an instant.

What should we say today, then, when the text itself has disappeared, when the proper names of the actors as well as of the authors are absent from the dictionary, when the places where the plays were performed have been destroyed, when we can no longer even imagine the public? When a whole tradition of theatre has suffered a shipwreck? Disappearance of the precariousness, organized oblivion of the creative oblivion, censoring of the instantaneous: what this book[1] seeks to restore to us is an engulfed continent of theatre. Engulfed, not for reasons of its own weaknesses – the reader, in any case, will be the judge of that – but because neither its existence nor its destination were inscribed in the plans of the powerful; engulfed for having tried to make theatre into the immediate auxiliary – at a minimum – of the consciousness of the workers in revolt and – at a maximum – of their political grassroots organization, the one that remains acceptable even to the anarchists: the 'immediacy' of trade unionism.

As we know since at least Thermidor, brutal repression has never been enough for the bourgeois victors, and especially not for the ferocious French bourgeoisie, whose feats include, in June 1848 and at the time of the Commune, the principal massacres of workers in history; with the war of 1914, a particularly absurd holocaust of young peasants thrown to the flames in the trenches; then, the most atrocious colonial wars, the most shameful capitulations to the invader; and, today, since at least the end of the 1970s, the most retrograde and servile dispositions of intellectuals with regard to the established order – that of finance, ostentatious wealth, corruption, and the humiliation of thought. On top of their material victories, most often obtained with the support of foreign reactionaries, the French bourgeoisie also demands that the intelligence of their

1. *Translator's Note*: Badiou is referring to the book for which the present chapter originally served as the preface, that is, the first in a three-volume critical and editorial project about anarchist and socialist 'combat theatre', selected and presented by Jonny Ebstein, Philippe Ivernel, Monique Surel-Tupin and Sylvie Thomas, *Au temps de l'anarchie: un théâtre de combat, 1880–1914* (Paris: Séguier-Archimbaud, 2001).

enemies in combat, to the extent that this is possible, be forbidden for future generations. They give their own moralistic, linear and inert version of History. They sift everything through their own deceptive system of values ('democracy', 'liberty', and so on) and transform their strongest and toughest adversaries – Robespierre or Marat, or Varlin, or Blanqui, or Louise Michel – either into bloody fanatics if they had the latitude to act, or into insignificant utopians if they were firmly controlled by the repressive apparatus. Today, especially, this type of historical revisionism is rife, with countless servile penpushers taking on the task of 'proving' that such or such a great figure of the spirit of insurrection was either a criminal or a dreamer or – this being the most delightful synthesis from the pens of these journalists of our reactionary times – a partisan of 'bloody utopias'. Not to mention, of course, the operations of suppression pure and simple, which can reach back far into the past: Is it not natural for François Furet's dictionary of the French Revolution to 'forget' the name of Saint-Just? But, after all, the official programs of the 'Republican' school have long forgotten, either in detail or nowadays as a whole, the Paris Commune.

The disappearance pure and simple of the anarchist or socialist theatre from the years 1880–1914 is only one arrangement among others in this endless settling of accounts of official history with whatever contradicts its norms and its judgements. This arrangement has been exceptionally effective. On this point, allow me to cite my own example. For the past ten years, in the margins of my philosophical or literary work and my activity as a militant, I endeavoured to write a few polemical plays about the contemporary world. In them I lined up the representatives of the world of politics (delegates, mayors, 'associationist' militants...); I invented situations that were simultaneously recognizable and incongruous; and I organized all this around a character whom I imagined to be the heir of the subtle slaves from ancient comedy, or the cunning valet of classical comedy: the proletarian Ahmed, of foreign origin, but who knows better than anyone the real inner workings of society in the metropolis. I thus put together, in the order of their composition, *Ahmed le subtil* (modeled upon Molière's *Les Fourberies de Scapin*), *Ahmed se fâche*, and *Ahmed philosophe*. The production of these plays, I might add, was taken up by a group of remarkable professional artists: Christian Schiaretti and his permanent troupe at the Comédie of Reims. Yet in spite of the excellent productions, we were never allowed to forget the ferociously and joyously critical dimension of our work, nor the massive counter-current that it represented in the face of the moralizing, compassionate, and apolitical orientation of the theatre that was dominant at the time. We obtained considerable public success in the most varied places, from Avignon to the obscure halls of some high school or local neighbourhood – a success that has not wavered (the plays are still being performed). There have been, and there still are almost every month, numerous reprises by amateur troupes all throughout France. The plays in question are frequently studied in elementary schools, when the teachers are looking for something that speaks to the real world of their students. As a result, extracts are published in a number of handbooks. But all this is to no avail: the critics remain silent en masse and, when the official connoisseurs of the 'milieu' draw up a balance sheet of the theatre from the last few years, nobody gives any place to this exceptional project. Not even, and I say this in all friendship, the authors of the introduction to the present book, when they rightly invoke the contemporary descendants of the authors they resuscitate, from Benedetto to Kergrist by way of Dario Fo.

I would thus have been particularly well-placed to appreciate the destiny of the combat theatre of the previous turn of the century, to reflect upon the silence in which this theatre was covered, to reread the plays, to consider myself as one of its legitimate heirs, in short: to participate in its resurrection.

And yet, nothing of the kind has happened. Because it was so well-organized, I have shared in the general ignorance, at the very time when in my own way I was its 'victim'. It was, after all, a question on the part of those who fabricate the public norms, of not taking into account anything from my attempt, just as it had been decided to make nothing, in the history of theatre, of the totality, or almost, of the attempt – both artistic and militant – of the anarchists.

I therefore greeted with particular enthusiasm (and a bit of shame, like the shame we feel when someone unexpectedly shows us something that we obviously ought to have known) the painstaking work of restitution led by Jonny Ebstein, Philippe Ivernel, Monique Surel-Tupin and Sylvie Thomas. I say with enthusiasm, but also with the recognition of someone who, appearances notwithstanding, detects a *sign of the times* in this kind of discovery that is both scholarly and nourished by a combatant certainty.

Indeed, we have been thrown into a long political and intellectual night by the reaction that followed the strong 1940s and no doubt culminated in the early 1980s – in France, in any case, this reaction did not level off until the movement of December 1995. But I do not think that this night is destined to last much longer, if it is not already starting to be undermined by a still undecided dawn. What this dawn will show, what it already shows, as witnessed in the present book, is that – within the limits of any historical analogy – our situation is closer to that of the second half of the nineteenth century than to the political heart of the twentieth, which comes after the October Revolution: after the era of communism established in the State, after the era of Stalin and the Third International, and even of what comes after World War II – the 'socialist camp' against the 'imperialist camp', the national liberation struggles, the great ideological youth movements. It is indeed the case that a certain revolutionary 'manner' has exhausted its virtues, having been consumed in the vain effort to master the inherent cruelty of the State with the alleged virtues of the working class party, or its substitutes. As far as I am concerned, I will never join the gang of those who argue on the basis of this sombre period so as to organize the large-scale abandonment, which they hope will be definitive, of all radical political ambition. To accept to draw some lessons from the past century only means to take up again the questions wherever the history of the different modes of politics left them. It means never to give up, always to continue, that is, to invent. But, beyond a vast effort of thought that, like that of Marx, goes to the root of things, these inventions once again suppose a completely new evaluation of what is, for our world, the figure of the worker and of the people, and where its political capacity might well come from. This is why the nineteenth century once again speaks to us in such a singular manner.

After the October Revolution, it was possible to think that two crucial questions of emancipatory political thinking had been settled: first, the economic base of emancipation means the collective appropriation of the means of production (by the State? therein lies the whole problem); and, second, the political form must be the authority (the dictatorship of the Party? therein, too, lies the whole problem) of the working class over society as a whole. Today, these strong hypotheses no longer have the force of conviction. The era in which they were invented, debated, combated, now puts other demands on us, for our own needs.

We could also say that capitalism and the political order that is proper to it (parliamentary 'democracy') present themselves once again, as was the case with the bourgeoisie and the petty bourgeoisie from the nineteenth century, as the sole natural economic and political configurations, with any other view of things being considered pathological. Around what we must have the courage to call bourgeois ideology, in the form of the restoration that it takes today, there exists a powerful consensus. Who, on the scene of what is visible in the media, contests property, inheritance, family, bourgeois juridical form, or the electoral and representational system? Who affirms the principle that political authority must return, not to the privileged and their scribes, but to the workers and the small and median salaried who, even though they are the crushing majority of the population, are practically kept out not only of the places of decision-making but also of all forms of representation, of the public image, or of positive self-valorization? Who still accepts the idea that to found true justice is certainly worth a bit of damage on the side of those who are well-off and their servants? And who, in the official theatre, can still find some drama in the evidence of these critical facts? In a political situation that is so mediocre, we must – like our anarchistic and socialist predecessors from after the Commune (a famous reactive period, too, those years between 1871 and 1880…) – use all the means at our disposal to begin to undermine the reactionary consensus. It is important to show that, far from being the natural form of collective life, liberal capitalism is an inegalitarian monstrosity. It is equally important to show that, far from being an acceptable form of democracy, the parliamentary system is its most insidious corruption, because it presents the continuation of oppression in the form of a rigged choice (the 'left' against the 'right', republicans against democrats, and so on). In sum, the point is to recreate the conditions for a veritable intellectual freedom.

The notion that theatre can and should contribute to this task is something of which I have always been convinced. But it is enormously encouraging to see the progressive intellectuals and militants from the end of the nineteenth century grappling with the same problem. It is particularly moving to observe, in the realm of theatrical projects, a mixture of writers whose name at least has been transmitted to us (Mirbeau or Georges Darien), writers from the period who have been forgotten (Jean Conti or Normandy), great historical figures (Louise Michel), key anarchist militants (Jean Grave or Charles Malato), and many others as well. This was indeed a vast movement, which furthermore had the courage that is now so rare to create a public of its own, and thus to assume that the price to pay for the autonomy of thought is the autonomy of the places of its expression. To imagine these sessions in Ménilmontant, so well discussed by the editors of this volume, where a large audience of workers and employees would listen to a powerful and unexpected melodrama, an intervention by Jean Jaurès, and the songs from the Commune, shows us the path to follow on at least one point: to know how to keep hold of the singularity of emancipation; to become, once again, indifferent to the official spectacle of society. We must convince ourselves that the political rupture is not a question of virulence in words, nor is it a matter of causing a superficial furore. It is a patient and thorough process, which builds its own figures and its immanent places, which sets its own dates, and which never lets the choice of space or time be dictated to it. Yes, there is always a need for propaganda, especially today, when the minds are so profoundly subjugated and corrupted.

But it follows a set of laws that are completely different from those of publicity. And this is precisely the reason why theatre, in all its continued greatness, can be a theatre of propaganda, whereas it can never be at the service of publicity. For theatre, too, patiently constructs unlikely figures, and it, too, can gather people on the margins of the metropolis. Any hall whatsoever, a table, a piece of cloth: as the anarchists and socialists of the end of the nineteenth century have shown to us, theatre can freely go in search of those who deserve the critical and violent forms of thought that it seeks to bear. Which is why it is irreplaceable.

Everything pertaining to these authors who for so long had been kept secret deserves to be meditated – including the genres they practiced. Fundamentally: the (naturalist?) melodrama and the (critical?) fable. The first exhibits a violent chunk of the popular real; the second parades around the puppets of ordinary oppression. This is truly the problem of every militant form of theatre, a problem upon which Brecht himself reflected for a long time: how to combine the *revelatory* function of political theatre (to show the inequality and the savagery of the oppressors) and its *mobilizing* function (to arouse the courage of the revolt, but also its methodicalness)? Even if some parts of the theatre published in this book are understandably hesitant on this point, we know that the melodramatic identification with the victims does not directly produce the political consciousness. We know all the same that the identification with the spontaneous but also deadly revolts (to die with the bomb still in one's hands, to commit suicide just as one kills the vile profiteer, and so on) does not advance the collective capacity for action. Finally, it is clear that the farcical presentation of the powerful, no matter how indispensable it may be, leaves completely open the question of the affirmative power that takes over from this derisory and sinister power. In order to balance these difficulties, Brecht needed to substitute distancing for identification (but in actual fact they are dialectically related), combine the praise of organization or of the party with that of the solitary consciousness of the revolt (but the party without revolt is nothing more than bureaucracy), show that oppression and the consciousness of oppression are two very different things (the theatricalization of this difference is a delicate process) and make limited use of the comical effect, so as to suggest that there is too much symmetry in the reversal, enacted by the farce, between the superiority of the powerful and the energy of the dominated.

At the end of the nineteenth century, when André Antoine uses the axioms of naturalism to innovate the theatre and when Chekhov and Stanislavski revolutionize its poetics and its technique, the anarchist writers have recourse to a much older heritage, in the contrasting forms of the melodrama (which goes back to the high years of the theatre of the boulevard) and of the farce of social types (close to the elliptical puppet theatre in Lyon). More so than in these techniques per se, the formal limit undoubtedly resides elsewhere. The real difficulty, which is considerable, consists in knowing how to emphasize the affirmation in the negation, how to reveal the political possibility in the showcasing of the abject, and how to define the hero, if not necessarily as 'positive' (this will be the cross of 'socialist realism'), then in any case as the bearer of an intelligence of the situations and a capacity for intervention that guarantee, beyond the *necessity* of the revolt delivered by the social criticism, the certainty of its *power*. This alone holds the key of the passage to politics, or – if one is more anarchist in formation – to lasting and thoughtful collective action. It is no doubt by stumbling upon this problem and because of the disjointed treatment it receives (melodramatic criticism, farcical intervention) that this theatre has failed, not in being great, courageous, or lively, but in creating lasting or even eternal figures such as the Slave (Sosie) or the Valet (Scapin), and as someone like the Proletarian deserves to be, whether in a drama or in a farce. It is true that to do so, as Scapin already showed, and as Chaplin's creation of the vagabond-critic would show soon afterward, this theatre would have to assume a complex form of thinking, within the 'anarchistic' subjectivity, as to the interlacing of Good and Evil, of solidarity and malice. It is only at this price that the corrosiveness of criticism can take on a universal value, and that the political propaganda can escape its intimate enemy, which is that of moral propaganda. This lesson is important to us, since the current form of reactionary ideological pressure also consists in calling upon us to be 'moral' (human rights, international tribunals, humanitarian interventions, and so on). The dissidence that we need will not be able to follow the path that often was the path chosen by the combat theatre of the nineteenth century, trained in this regard by its true literary master who remains the immense figure of Victor Hugo – the Hugo of *Les Misérables* or of *Cent mille francs de récompense*. This was the path in which the humble had the right to declare to the rich and powerful: 'We are more moral than you.' We must come to understand the theatrical desire for such a right, while at the same time acknowledging that it is no longer available, or even welcome, for us today. Indeed what we need is to impose a sovereign gap between political (or social) justice and the holy water font in which the contemporary catechisms are soaked. This is why the hero of the theatre of liberation will have no use for morality and no doubt will be beyond Good and Evil.

All these questions seem to leave today's theatre indifferent, all devoted as it is to the choruses that with their deploring formulas pretend to express the morality of the miseries of this world, without describing or even naming the great mechanism whose superb functioning the truly liberating action must derail, if only on a single point. But just as we will soon enough return to the decisive questions of equality or of a politics of the working and popular figure, so too will the theatre rediscover what always was its function: to let shine the critical intelligence of a public without frontiers. In this regard, and aided by the experience of having gone through the legacy of Brecht and his descendants, it is important to reread the colourful, courageous and independent theatre that this book proposes to us. As long as we will not have done as much – and more – in terms of works and publics as these militant artists, we will have to say that we are still being schooled by them.

4

NOTES ON JEAN-PAUL SARTRE'S *THE CONDEMNED OF ALTONA*

1. When I first saw *Les Séquestrés d'Altona* (*The Condemned of Altona*, also known as *Loser Wins*) upon its creation in 1959, I was struck by the contrast between the dramatic splendour of certain passages – all attributable to the role of Franz – and the thickness of almost everything else, its melodramatic abstraction, the slowness of its procedures. Serge Reggiani, playing a memorable Franz, often seemed to perform a play within the play – a good play within a less good one – with an intrinsic brilliance that seemed to leave the other actors on stage in the role of atonal spectators.

2. But, after all, is this not what the play demands? Sequestered in a room for the past thirteen years, Franz plays a role, for himself as much as for the others – the role of the witness of History, and even of Humanity: 'Man is dead, and I am his witness', he says in the alleged tribunal of the Crabs, those 'masked inhabitants of the ceilings', the species that he imagines has succeeded, in the thirtieth century, the dead

humanity.[1] The fact that he is playing a role (the meaning of which will gradually become clear in the play) is something that Franz's incestuous sister Leni tells him to his face ('Masked inhabitants of the ceiling, the witness of the centuries is a false witness'),[2] as does his sister-in-law Johanna, from whom Franz will wait in vain for a lying redemption: 'You're a fake, right to the marrow of your bones.'[3] The splendid perorations of Franz about the Century, about Man, about Culpability, are just so many performances behind which an unnameable truth is hidden, the one that Johanna will no longer be able to tolerate, the one about which – though always ready to lie to her – he told her: 'I shall renounce my illusions when … I love you more than my lies, and when you love me in spite of my truth.'[4] In this sense, it is only fair that the fallacious brilliance of Franz's discourse would be exposed before ordinary witnesses. The madness of the century is shown in the confrontation with the dreariness of the life of these men and women who continue to live as if there were nothing more to it.

3. Still, there are three plays tangled up in these five interminable acts, with each one trying to carry the other two. What takes so much laborious effort are these exercises of carrying and being carried away. This is what takes the life out of the play: to my knowledge (which no doubt is imperfect), it has rarely (or never?) been produced again after its creation, contrary to that dramatic heavyweight in Sartre's oeuvre, *Le Diable et le Bon Dieu* (*The Devil and the Good Lord*), which is still

---

1. Jean-Paul Sartre, *The Condemned of Altona: A Play in Five Acts*, trans. Sylvia and George Leeson (New York: Alfred A. Knopf, 1961), p. 58.
2. Ibid., p. 70.
3. Ibid., p. 132.
4. Ibid.

on today. And yet, people read this burdensome piece of dramatic junk – this ambitious, meandering, failed and gripping play.

4. First, a familial melodrama. That of the family of the Von Gerlachs, duly centred on the link between the Father and the Son (no Mother whatsoever in this arid landscape). Sartre does not hide his allegories: in the list of characters, the father is simply called 'Father'. Everything starts from this symbol.

5. Let us tell the story. An industrialist (the head of a major shipyard in Hamburg) has three children: two sons, Franz and Werner, and one daughter, Leni. He has been unharmed all through the experiences of Nazism, World War II, the destruction of the cities, and then the American reconstruction of this (unlikely) Germany to which Sartre invites us. Thanks to his influence on the successive powers that be, this is a man who has always managed to fix all shady affairs, his own as well as those of his favourite son, Franz, who in his eyes, despite the fact that he apparently has gone mad, is 'the last of the *true* Von Gerlachs'.[5] For some mysterious reason, shortly after the end of the war, in 1946, Franz locked himself up in his room, where he is still ruminating. The other son, Werner, who is an honourable lawyer, has married a very pretty woman, Johanna, a starlet whose career, for reasons that are equally obscure, has not really taken off. Leni, the daughter, always sarcastic and well-established in the role – to speak with Hegel – of the irony of the (familial) community,[6] loves her brother Franz,

5. Ibid., p. 22.

6. *Translator's Note*: Hegel speaks of woman as 'the everlasting irony of the community' with regard to the role of Antigone in the tragedy of Sophocles. See G. W. F. Hegel, 'The Ethical Order', *The Phenomenology of Spirit*, trans. A. V. Miller (Oxford: Clarendon Press,

takes care of him, sleeps with him (this incest, by the way, is one of the work's weakest and most abstract elements). This small world lives cloistered in an immense house (twenty-two rooms!) in the distant suburb of Hamburg that is Altona. At the start of the first act, the most trying exercise of exposition that one has ever seen in the theatre, the father has just found out that he is about to die of throat cancer. He names Werner his heir at the helm of the family business, against the wish of his spouse Johanna, who does not want to see her marriage sequestered forever in the sinister home of the Gerlachs. But what this father desires above all is to see his son Franz again: the principal condemned, whom he has not seen in person for thirteen years, but whose every step and dream he spies on at night. First, he bypasses Leni's guardianship by having his daughter-in-law go up to the madman's room, under the pretense of her beauty (which equals absence, negation). Then, he undoes the love for Franz that takes hold of Johanna (to the point where she considers remaining locked up with him), by making Leni reveal Franz's shameful secret. After which the road to the reencounters is wide open, coinciding with death: both father and son, the first in despair over the empty fact of death, and the second in despair over the fact that Johanna has judged him to be guilty – thus making him lose his trial against History – commit suicide by driving their Porsche into the river.

6. We thus obtain the following: the dialectic of symbolic enslavement and deadly deliverance of the Father and the Son (Franz, speaking about the father: 'He created me in his image – unless he has become the image of what

---

1977), p. 287. For a famous criticism, see Luce Irigaray, 'The Eternal Irony of the Community', in *Speculum of the Other Woman*, trans. Gillian Gill (Ithaca, NY: Cornell University Press, 1985).

he created');[7] the capacity for judgement attributed to Beauty: this is the Achilles heel of the sequestered, about whom the father says melancholically that 'he used to love beauty' and who will open his door to Johanna, for reasons that he promptly explains himself: 'The trick brought nothing into the room, that's all. Emptiness, a diamond that cuts no glass, an absence, beauty'; the irony of incest (Leni: 'I don't amount to anything, but I was born a Gerlach, which means I am mad with pride – and I cannot make love to anyone but a Gerlach. Incest is my law and my fate. (*Laughing.*) It's my way of strengthening the family ties'); the hell of conjugality (Werner: 'And how could I have lost you, Johanna I have never had you. ... You cheated me on the deal. I wanted a wife, and I've only possessed her corpse'); the impossibility of redemption by love alone and, more generally, the anonymous impasse of the relationship between men and women (Johanna: 'Any woman is still good enough for any man'); the totalizing function of death (Franz's father, before their suicide: 'I made you, I will unmake you. My death will envelop yours, and in the end I shall be the only one to die'); the family as generalized neurosis, the exteriority of the Truth as soon as we are caught on the merry-go-round of the different roles. It is also the father who states this: 'In the family, you see, we have no objection to the truth. But whenever possible we contrive to have it spoken by a stranger'. And Werner: 'There's no tree without a rotten branch'.[8]

7. In sum, with all this we could make a passably good Ibsen play, though it would be too complicated. Or an honourable Pirandello play, though too simple, this time.

---

7. Sartre, *The Condemned of Altona*, p. 80.
8. Ibid., pp. 54, 78, 88, 115, 55, 174, 18, 114.

8. But there is the second play: a moral fable, the core of which concerns the sempiternal question, both for Sartre (who makes it into the motif, as early as 1941, of his play *Morts sans sépulture*) and for many others, of torture. In reality this is what makes *The Condemned* into a play directly marked by the liveliest actuality. In 1959, we are still in the midst of the war in Algeria. For years we have known that the French army systematically tortures prisoners, suspects, and anybody who looks like an Arab; and that the police do the same, including in police stations back in Paris. Already, some young recruits desert rather than become mixed up in this kind of horror. The polemic on this topic will increasingly become the ideological issue of the moment that drives a wedge between the intellectuals. If Sartre's Germany is evasive, if his Nazis, his officers from the Wehrmacht, or even after the war his industry bosses seem to be so disembodied, it is because at least one of the three plays contained in *The Condemned* (the familial melodrama, the moral fable, and the theory of the relations between the individual and History) finds its subject-matter in the crucial choices that the French faced at the end of the 1950s.

9. Let us do some more storytelling. Franz's moral itinerary involves three primitive scenes, three 'situations', as Sartre the philosopher would have said. First, in the spring of 1941, Himmler's services purchase a vast piece of land from father Gerlach. The plan is to use this land to build a concentration camp. From this camp, one day, a Polish rabbi escapes. Franz hides him in his room. The father phones Goebbels to take care of the affair. We won't know, incidentally, whether by doing so he has put himself in the role of informer. A chauffeur for the family, an open Nazi, is suspected of knowing about the situation and has disappeared into the village,

but nothing is sure: such is the regime of ambiguities in which Sartre plunges the figure of the father. In any case, the Nazi henchmen arrive at the house and, with four of them holding Franz down, slaughter the rabbi before the latter's eyes. The experience is threefold: experience of the moral imperative (to protect the victim at all cost); experience of symbolic dependency (only the father can settle the affair, if it can be settled, but in the end he really does not settle it); experience of the practical impotence of morality: the bestial force annihilates the actuality of the Good.

The second primitive scene, which is also the most complex and about which we will not hear the truth until the end of the play, directly concerns torture. Following the episode of the rabbi, Franz is sent to the Russian front. Near Smolensk, the partisans surround his detachment. Some peasants are imprisoned. Heinrich, a low-ranked officer and a real brute, with ample support from his soldiers, proposes that they torture the prisoners in order to obtain information about the partisans. At first (and according to the version of the story that he tells to Johanna), Franz refuses absolutely. As a result, he finds himself guilty for the almost complete annihilation of his section – in the name of what? 'Principles, my dear, always principles. You can guess that I preferred my own soldiers to those two unknown prisoners. Nevertheless, I had to say no. … He who does not do all does nothing. I did nothing. He who has done nothing is nobody.'[9] But this accusation of irresponsibility in the name of principles, which Franz calls 'the most important point of the indictment',[10] is only a decoy. In reality, in order not to be brought back to the experience of powerlessness (four soldiers holding him back, and Heinrich tortures the peasants before his eyes), Franz

9. Ibid., p. 148.
10. Ibid.

himself has personally engaged in torture, using his pen-knife and cigarette lighter, even if it was to no avail: the peasants died without saying a word. This experience, which is that of absolute Evil apparently inscribed in a superior duty ('We should have won the war. By any means – I said by *any*, see?'),[11] is the reason why Franz pleads endlessly before the court of the Crabs, trying to have himself absolved by the centuries to come by making his own century responsible.

The third situation leads us back to the acts that are in vain, because the father twists their meaning and their consequences. Leni, with her perverse sense of irony, right after the war has got into the habit of leading on the American officers who occupy the house, only to go on declaring herself to be a Nazi whereas they would be nothing but dirty Jews. One of the officers, in his anger, has attempted to rape her. Franz intervenes and the American is struck with a bottle. Franz takes all the blame, once again to no avail, since the father, who is just as close to the occupying General Hopkins as he was before to Goebbels, settles the whole affair: Franz will leave for Argentina, and nothing more will be said about all this. This time around, though, Franz shows reluctance. He refuses to leave and locks himself up for thirteen years in his room, alone before the 'masked inhabitants of the ceiling'.

10. There we have a summary of the questions for which Sartre, all through his life, nourished the project of a moral philosophy of a new type.[12] Taking into account

---

11. Ibid., p. 86.

12. *Translator's Note*: For some of Sartre's posthumously published notes that pick up on this project for a new moral philosophy, first announced in the conclusion to *Being and Nothingness*, see Jean-Paul Sartre, *Notebooks for an Ethics*, trans. David Pellauer (Chicago: University of Chicago Press, 1992).

the determined nature of situations (the chain of means and ends to win a war, the symbolic dependency on the Father, the uncontrollable infinity of consequences...), how can I assure that my act amounts to the universal affirmation of human freedom? Since in any case I am responsible for the meaning attributed to my situation, how can I distinguish a meaning that conforms to the humanity of the human being (Good) from a meaning that ratifies the inevitable inhumanity of the human beast (Evil)? How can I reach the transparency of the (self-)consciousness of my act, given that this act is always staged for so and so? If, for example, Franz expects redemption from Johanna's loving judgement, how can he not lie to her on the subject of torture? If he tells her the truth, does this not amount to choosing the perpetuation of the situation and turning away from the possibility of a meaning that would organize a genuinely different future? But if he lies to her, is that not also a way of subtracting himself from the judgement that on the other hand he begs for? If death lies on both sides of a decision, what tips the balance? Torturing the prisoners means giving the soldiers a chance to escape. Not torturing them means leading them into disaster. Where is, in this situation, the norm of the choice? Should we not therefore change registers and exculpate the individual so as to bring action against History? Should morality not leave the subjects who share a common destiny in a state of inseparation (Franz: 'I will save the world as a whole, but I will not help anyone in particular')?[13] For a materialist, is powerlessness not the worst of all options, leading back to the moral philosophy of Kant's formalism? This is indeed what pushes Franz in the end to assume torture, knowing full well that it is something that nobody can assume: 'I shall never again fall into

13. Sartre, *The Condemned of Altona*, p. 77.

abject powerlessness. … I'll assume the evil; I'll display my power by the singularity of an unforgettable act; change *living* men into vermin.'[14] And yet, is it really the case that, in doing so, the executioner decides 'life or death', as Franz bitterly claims? After all, as his father remarks, those peasants did not talk under the effects of torture, 'it was they who decided life or death.'[15] But is this not because they were on the good side? And is it not always possible to rejoin this alleged 'good side' in the conflicts of History?

11. The theatrical formalization of these questions is organized in the space of the trial. A suspect, a witness, a charge, a judge…: such are the rotating places that the characters can come to occupy, one after the other. Franz's complex stratagem consists in presenting himself as witness (or even as lawyer) of an entity much vaster than he (the Century, History, Man…), whereas the source of everything is his flagrant personal guilt: he has tortured, which confirms absolutely the beast inside man. The legitimacy of the construction of that superior entity is the topic of the third play within the play: the individual and History. But already at the most elementary level of the moral judgement regarding Franz's acts, we realize that this construction is not possible without a series of falsifications that authorize one to have reasonable doubts. Thus, in order to put on the same level the Nazis (and thus his own atrocities) and their adversaries, which allows him to condemn History, Franz must pretend to believe that the Allies have annihilated Germany, that to the genocide of the Jews there corresponds a genocide of the Germans: 'Judges? Have they never pillaged, massacred, and raped? Was it Goering who dropped the bomb on Hiroshima? If they judge

14. Ibid., p. 164.
15. Ibid.

us, who will judge them? They speak of our crimes in order to justify the crime they are quietly preparing – the systematic extermination of the German people.' He demands, first of Leni and then of Johanna, that they confirm him in this false 'belief'. Johanna obliges, lovingly, as in a mad delusion: 'A double delirium – very well. (*Pause.*) Germany is on its deathbed.' But in spite of these false witnesses, Franz is not duped by his own artifice: 'I pretended that I was locking myself up so that I shouldn't witness Germany's agony. It's a lie. I wanted my country to die, and I shut myself up so that I shouldn't be a witness to its resurrection.'[16] Franz searches for a judge who would be beyond doubt, without ever considering that this judge might quite simply pronounce his personal guilt. The play then unfolds the stages in this impossible quest for a *legitimate* verdict. There is first the court of the Crabs, before which Franz pleads with great self-assurance for his acquittal: 'Decapods… We plead not guilty. … Centuries, I shall tell you how my century tasted, and you will acquit the accused.' But the Crabs are mute. Then there is Johanna, before whom the question promptly becomes that of truth: 'When I look at you, I know that truth exists and that it's not on my side.' For her, he will dismantle the tribunal of the Crabs: 'Johanna, I challenge their competence. I take the matter out of their hands, and I pass it over to you. Judge me.' After having heard the first (false) version of the story about the torture in Smolensk, Johanna declares: 'I acquit you.' After a second version, spilled by Leni, she can no longer save either her love or Franz. It is 'in a kind of terror', as the stage directions read, that she finds out that he has engaged in torture. She will not say another word to him. Then comes the one who has always been the organizer and the judge on duty:

16. Ibid., pp. 30, 95, 165.

the father. After telling him, 'You won't be my judge,' and then, 'I think you are judging me, aren't you?' Franz arrives at his eternal demand: 'Judge me!' accompanied by the observation: 'Informer or no informer, you're my natural judge.' But there can be no 'natural' judge, and the Father's verdict will be that, with all these theatrical trials, Franz has created pure nothingness: 'Both your life and your death are merely *nothing*. You are nothing, you do nothing, you have done nothing, and you can do nothing.'[17] In part falling back on the romantic nihilism that never ceased haunting Sartre, the play near its end relies on the voice of the Father to pronounce that the Son is neither guilty nor innocent, simply for lack of being.

12. In the 1940s and 1950s, such nihilistic constructions embedded within the tragedy of Good and Evil were very common in France, in cinema – the great filmic trials of Cayatte – as well as in theatre: Anouilh, the endless debate between powerless purity and disgusting reality (*Mademoiselle Colombe, Antigone, Romeo and Jeannette*...), or Montherlant, the confrontation between power and nothingness (*La Reine morte, Malatesta*...).[18] Sartre remains close to this current, which probably explains why he never brought innovation to the form

17. Ibid., pp. 58, 131, 133, 148, 160–1, 165, 171.

18. *Translator's Note*: André Cayatte (1909–1989) was a French filmmaker of the New Wave, author of movies such as *Justice est faite* (*Justice is Done*, 1950) and *Nous sommes tous des assassins* (*We Are All Murderers*, 1952). Jean Anouilh (1910–1967) was one of France's most famous dramatists. Both *Antigone* (1944) and *Roméo et Jeannette* (1946) have been translated in Jean Anouilh, *Plays*, vol. 1 (New York: Hill & Wang, 1958). *Colombe*, first performed in 1951, was translated by Louis Kronenberger as *Mademoiselle Colombe* (New York: Coward-McCann, 1954). Henry de Montherlant (1895–1972) was a controversial French essayist, novelist, and playwright. *La Reine morte* (*The Dead Queen*) is from 1934; *Malatesta* was first performed in 1950 and is still frequently produced today.

of theatre, why he never was able to erase the traces of the 'intellectual boulevard'. Nevertheless, the doublet of the familial melodrama and the morality trial is supplanted and overcome by the third play within the play, which in terms of its content is rather evocative of the early Brecht of *In the Jungle of Cities* or *Baal*. Indeed, this time around, what we obtain on the brink of madness is a decontextualized meditation on History and Subjectivity.

13. Let us tell the story. Locked up, fed and loved by Leni, the sole living being he still accepts to see, Franz pleads endlessly for his century (the twentieth): first before a tribunal from the thirtieth century, whose judges are no longer men but Crabs; then before Johanna, and even before the father. As he will later tell Johanna, not without a sense of humour: 'You must know that the human race started off on the wrong foot, but I put the lid on its fabulous ill-fortune by handing over its mortal remains to the Court of the Crustaceans.'[19] The maximal aim of his defence plea – or his testimony – is to obtain his acquittal, in light of the fact that the countless crimes committed by men have been due to the century, to its general texture, and not due to the singular malice of any of those men. The century did not really *produce* Evil, it constantly came upon Evil as the bloody inertia from which it was necessary to start in order to do Good. 'Evil, your lordships, evil was the only material we had. We worked on it in our refineries, and the finished product became good. Result: the good turned bad. And don't run away with the idea that the evil turned out well.' What happened in the twentieth century is that man has found himself in the guise of the beast that he also is: 'The century might have been a good one had not man

19. Sartre, *The Condemned of Altona*, p. 133.

been watched from time immemorial by the cruel enemy who had sworn to destroy him, that hairless, evil, flesh-eating beast – man himself.' The maximum goal is for the century, at least, not to be denied, for it not to be suppressed, for it to count for the times that are still to come: 'Don't throw my century into the ashcan.' Or again: 'Take care, you judges; if I rot, my century will be engulfed. The flock of the centuries needs a black sheep. What will the fortieth say, Arthropods, if the twentieth has wandered from the fold?'[20]

But this general plea is only the first strand in Franz's vaticination. As we saw before, this could equally well be an artifice meant to absolve, in the name of an anonymous culpability, the singular crimes that he has committed. The second level is when Franz claims for himself the responsibility of everything that has occurred in the century. By a kind of inversion, the century, which served as the objective support in the trial of mankind, becomes immanent, with Franz as its bearer as much as any other man. The witness of the century on trial becomes coextensive with that to which he bears witness. Man no longer is dead, as he pretended before the Crabs: he is the living witness of his own general ignominy. This conversion intervenes when Franz changes tribunals and exposes himself to Johanna: 'The witness for mankind... And who should that be? Come, madame, it's mankind. A child could guess that. The accused testifies for himself. I see that there is a vicious circle.'

To assume this 'vicious circle' amounts to making the century into the burden of every singular man. It amounts to presenting at one and the same time the defence of the century and the defence of one's personal decisions. A reciprocity of meaning, and even of existence, is established between historic universality and

20. Ibid., pp. 74, 177, 74.

intimate destiny. Whence Franz's declarations that are both emphatic and decisive: 'I'm carrying the centuries on my back, and if I straighten up they will crash' and 'I'll take responsibility for the war as though I were carrying it on alone, and then, when I've won, I'll sign up again.' Finally, the declaration that concludes the play: 'I, Franz von Gerlach, here in this room, have taken the century upon my shoulders and have said: 'I will answer for it. This day and forever.'[21]

14. This beautiful text is spoken by a tape recorder, on an empty stage, after the hero's suicide. Sartre introduces this apparatus as the technical witness of the witness by which, in a rare move, he is being innovative. Just as the hero in Beckett's *Krapp's Last Tape*, with which *The Condemned of Altona* maintains a connection that is both secret and paradoxical, Franz collects the tapes of his woolly pleas. He is the archivist of the century, at the same time as he is its witness, its judge, and its paradigmatic guilty party.

15. But perhaps it is the weak Werner, that self-effacing and annoying character, who holds the true maxim of all this pathos. His weakness is something that his father – *the* father, who is also a cheap Nietzschean – pronounces in the sentence: 'Werner is weak, Franz is strong. That can't be helped.' But Werner rejects this distribution of roles and declares himself homogenous with human universality: 'I am like any other man. Neither strong nor weak, and, like anyone else, I am trying to live.'[22] The force of this anonymous 'weakness' lies in the fact that it serves as the vehicle for a fundamental truth – the equality of all human beings:

21. Ibid., pp. 133, 121, 145, 178.
22. Ibid., p. 24.

Werner: When I look a man in the eyes I become incapable of giving him orders.
Father: Why?
Werner: I feel that he is my equal.[23]

And, no doubt, what keeps nihilism at bay and allows everyone honourably to carry the century on his or her shoulders is indeed the capacity to remain faithful, as much as possible, to the egalitarian maxim.

16. Franz's voice, at the end: 'I surprised the beast. I struck. A man fell, and in his dying eyes I saw the beast still living – myself. One and one make one.'[24]

Yes, 'one and one make one', there exists no transcendent discrimination between Beast and Man. But what counts is something else: every one counts for one. Each One is one. Whence the possible existence – therein lies the whole being of truth – of a generic multiplicity. For this kind of multiplicity, though, one cannot be 'responsible', which is why I keep my distance from Sartre. One can only be its militant. This is the theatrical distance travelled between the reflective confinement and the decision. Or: *The Decision*, a play by Brecht.[25]

17. Something in Sartre's theatre, in spite of its great merits, its historical good will, its grandeur and its brilliance, is irreparably pre-Brechtian. As when one says 'pre-war'.

---

23. Ibid., p. 10.

24. Ibid., p. 178.

25. *Translator's Note*: For more on Brecht's 1930 play *The Decision*, see Alain Badiou, *The Century*, trans. Alberto Toscano (Cambridge: Polity, 2007), pp. 119–22; and on the gradual distancing or detachment from Sartre, see Alain Badiou, 'Commitment, Detachment, Fidelity', in *The Adventure of French Philosophy*, trans. Bruno Bosteels (London: Verso, 2012), pp. 27–37.

5

THE AHMED TETRALOGY

I

'Ahmed' for me was first of all the name of a childhood, a solitude, a politics and a chance.

Childhood. In the lyceum, under the direction of an exceptional teacher who was a mixture of sweet-natured madness and enlightenment, I had played in Molière's *Les Fourberies de Scapin* (*Scapin's Deceits*). Being launched, at the age of sixteen, onto the forecourt of a small castle, with a baton in one's hand, is something that leaves deep traces. All the more so in that my first felt emotion in the theatre, some years before, was tied to these same *Fourberies*, produced by the company Le Grenier in Toulouse, with Daniel Sorano in the title role, who would go on to become one of Jean Vilar's steadiest collaborators. What took hold around this play was the conjunction of a young man and a strong sequence in the history of theatre in France, the one marked by decentralization and the rise of 'popular' theatre. I was to be haunted forever by Scapin. The fact that this haunting would eventually take the form of a rewriting of Molière's play (this is the case of my *Ahmed le subtil*) shows the distant effects of childhood infatuations and how, no matter how incalculable the forms and lengths of their influence, we are bound to remain faithful to them.

Solitude. In the fall of 1984 I find myself alone in the countryside, not far from the city of Toulouse where I spent my childhood and played Scapin. Solitude expands time to infinity, with the admixture of a slight anxiety, so that even all the powers of working and dreaming do not suffice to fill the hours and transfer the anxiety onto some saving symbol. I had nothing in the works at the time in the domain of philosophy. My *Theory of the Subject* was still recent (1982) and the manuscript for *Peut-on penser la politique?* (*Can Politics Be Thought?*) was finished. In one fell swoop, a bit like an intense memory that grips you, a childhood memory, as one speaks of a childhood flame, I threw myself on *Les Fourberies de Scapin* and, scene by scene and line by line, took on its transposition onto a contemporary suburb or *banlieue*, with Ahmed as the hero, the master of intrigues, of language, and of the stick. The play was finished in two weeks, in a suspicious attack of enthusiasm nearly burned up by cigarettes. I nevertheless checked this outburst with regular mailings of certain scenes to friends of mine, and the testimony that I received from them about their astounding hilariousness indicated to me that I was not too far from the right track.

Politics. The same summer of 1984 is marked by a series of measures and abuses of power aimed at those who in the official discourse are called 'immigrants' and who are quite simply the proletarians of our modern cities. A few squalid shooters lying in ambush behind their windows had gunned down a group of young Arabs under the pretext that they were making noise;

policemen in total impunity had emptied their revolvers on a few boisterous kids from the suburbs; and, with all kinds of persecutory searches and controls, the government tried to limit, or even to prevent, the exercise of that elementary right of all workers, whatever their origin, which is to bring their family to where they live and work. The cold political determination that these base acts brought out in me also naturally found its way into the writing of *Ahmed le subtil*: not in the form of any ideological preaching but in the freedom that I granted myself to '*farcir*' (in the sense of 'to make farcical');[1] in the sovereign force of affirmation that I attributed to all those who were thus being hunted down – and whom I knew from having been a militant alongside them for a long time; and in the laughable excitement that overcame all the local politicians, in a cheerful confusion of both Left and Right.

Chance. This year – 1984 – was no ordinary year in the history of my relations with the theatre. In July of that year, at the Festival in Avignon, *L'Écharpe rouge* – an opera for which I had written the script – had been brought to the stage. The story behind this event is crucial, complex, and delayed. *L'Écharpe rouge* had first been a book, published in 1979, under the generic rubric of '*romanopéra*' (novel-opera). It was a giant fresco, copied from Claudel's *Satin Slipper*, in which the Catholic backdrop was replaced by the complete set of revolutionary references from the twentieth century. One could find in it the workers' insurrections, the peasant uprisings, the wars of national liberation, the conflicts within the Party, the student revolts, the repressions and the intrigues, the endless sacrifices and impasses of the power of the State. All of this mixed in with the

1. *Translator's Note*: In French, *farcir* means literally 'to stuff' or 'to cram', as in *tomates farcies*, 'stuffed tomatoes'. Badiou here is punning on the echoes with the theatrical farce.

powerful feelings of love and carried by a variable style that alternated parody and lyricism in great rhythmic 'medleys', heavy with imagery and reminiscences. Later on I called this composite work 'the transparent tomb of Marxism-Leninism'. At the time I had sent it randomly to some theatre people whom I admired. Antoine Vitez was extremely taken by the work and called me up to tell me so. This was the beginning of many years of intense proximity to this admirable man. He proposed that I transform *L'Écharpe rouge* into the script for an opera and to entrust Georges Aperghis with the music, while he would take on the theatrical direction. The result was a unique and surprising project, one that ran completely counter to the spirit of the time – in the early 1980s – rife with denials of our revolutionary commitments and with everyone rallying to parliamentary liberalism. The spectacle was magnificent, combining the ludic energy of Aperghis's phrasing with a stage setting by Yannis Kokkos which, aside from a mobile castle that transformed the figures on stage into near-marionettes, included large-scale slide projections that enchanted the tragedy with the nocturnal poetry of its deep and somber reds. Antoine Vitez gave his mise en scène the vivacity and stature of a legend. I was still under the impression of the emotion that the event of this performance in Avignon – a heavenly gift of art – awoke in me when I wrote *Ahmed le subtil*. I could not have imagined that a few years later my friend Antoine Vitez would suffer a sudden death. At the time he was the director of the Comédie-Française and he had plans to direct, precisely, this *Ahmed* of which, in 1987, he had offered a public reading of such virtuosity that he had the audience cry with laughter. His death, which I still occasionally put into doubt so as to lead a better life, distanced me from the theatre for a long period of time. *Ahmed le subtil* would lie dormant in the drawer. Such are the chances of life, the encounters; and such are the chances of death, the losses.

II

Among the people in the audience during Vitez's reading from *Ahmed le subtil* was Jean-Pierre Jourdain, then his collaborator at the National Theatre of Chaillot, charged in particular with programming and publications. In the early 1990s, Jean-Pierre Jourdain became the general secretary to Christian Schiaretti, a young theatre director whose style, concept and will to associate an author with the collective project of the theatre, in sum, everything seemed to him to go in the same direction as the theatricality of *Ahmed le subtil*. Jourdain passed on the manuscript to Christian Schiaretti, who confirmed his diagnostic. The chances of life, the unlikely encounters, once again took the upper hand. Not without the impression of facing my deceased friend, I too offered a public reading of my play, in the bar of the Comédie in Reims. Oh! It was childhood all over again! In the midst of streaming laughter, I once again became Scapin! Schiaretti had been preparing for this contemporary creation for a long time. He had worked on the style of the farce, and gathered the comedians best suited for the disciplined and frontal relation that the farce imposes between the stage and the audience. One of his strokes of genius was the decision to give a mask to Ahmed, asking Erhard Stiefel to sculpt an original mask especially for the occasion: a mask which, it is no exaggeration to say, is an absolute masterpiece. Thus, Ahmed was no longer just any 'immigrant' from realism. Instead, through the power of language, the intrigues, the free and material affirmation of the superiority of the spirit, he became the heir of all those characters through whom comedy and the farce that is its essence bring to light the revenge of the people 'from below', and fictionalize the indestructible desire to exist that animates their watchful intelligence. Around Ahmed, you had the two camps, barefaced: on the one hand, the youth – indolent and bullied, always hoping to fix things with the least possible effort; and, on the other, the tiny personalities of the notables: the communist Mayor Lanterne, the reactionary representative Madame Pompestan, the fascistic foreman Moustache, the cultural coordinator and union organizer Rhubarbe – all figures reduced to their verbal tics, their obtuse energy, and their mutilated view of the situation. This allows Ahmed, master of his own desire, to put to his advantage even the contempt that these petty socialites nurse for him, so as to pull a fast one on them. On the stage all this took on a heavy and melancholic air, which revealed the two sides to Ahmed's solitude: his inventive genius, of which nobody knows the origin, and the absence of any genuine gratefulness, when he is done mixing and then unraveling all the threads of the plot. This is why the performances of *Ahmed le subtil* by the Comédie of Reims, during the Festival of Avignon in 1994, in the Parisian region in 1995, as well as during a long run in the provinces, were a huge popular success, whereas the critics frowned upon the play – ill-prepared as they were for this direct, luminous, affirmative and language-oriented theatre in which the classical tradition (literary as much as theatrical) was combined with the most radical contemporaneity.

A masked hero, recognizable theatrical types, tried and tested formulas from the farcical tradition…: It is time that we say what this 'Ahmed project' owes to the *commedia dell'arte*. My answer is: Nothing, precisely because without nostalgia or pointless memory, it seeks to do for the theatre today what the Italian theatre did three centuries ago. In the Ahmed cycle (which finally is comprised of four plays: *Ahmed le subtil*, *Ahmed philosophe*, *Ahmed se fâche* and *Les Citrouilles*), there is no citation, not even an imitation, of figures such as Harlequin, Pantalon, Colombine ... There is the explicit will to create contemporary theatrical types whose solidity and flexibility would be comparable to them, but with entirely different desires and situations. I will give just one example. An essential feature of the Italian types is their voracity, or their appetite – as much for food as for sex and money. The result is that the body's energy constantly trumps the verbal virtuosity, so that the 'large canvas' is the most appropriate literary form. It is true that Ahmed and all the types around him dispose of an appropriate bodily or visual 'instrument': Ahmed is an athlete of the stage, well-versed in the discipline of the mask, supple and fast; Madame Pompestan is a haughty transvestite, with neither vulgarity nor complacency; Rhubarbe is a ponderous bigmouth dressed in corduroy pants and with a pipe hanging from his lips; Moustache is a fat pig in a teddy, always ready for a brawl; Fenda, an attractive African woman à la 'island bird'; Camille, a hooligan in leather jacket. The costume designer in Reims, Annika Nilsson, had created costumes that were both timeless and characteristic of each type. Ahmed's black cape and his red and gold jacket; Madame Pompestan's green (or purple) tailored suit; Fenda's astounding baby-blue boubou; Rhubarbe's black corduroy jacket and his ruff: everything functions as a signal, on the border between a reminiscence from the seventeenth century and the capture, more symbolic than realist, of today's social pretentions. However, the question for these characters was not primarily their simple survival in a world of starvation, nor their concern for appearances. The real question is that of their capacity, in the world such as it is, and ultimately this capacity can be measured by their idiom, by the possibility for language to name their desire, to designate their enemies, and to fool them with a superior intelligence. Even the ridiculous notables are first of all characterized by their jargon. So the bodies must be at the service of language, and not the other way around: whether it is a stereotypical and restricted language, whose comic effect stems from the fact that it is flung back and forth with all the more conviction, the more it fails to relate to anything real (Lanterne, Pompestan, Rhubarbe); or an impoverished and powerless language, which is frustrated by this powerlessness without discerning its origin (the youth); or a brutal language entirely composed of the dregs of resentment (Moustache); or finally a diagonal language, the one that juggles with all the available resources and all the subtleties, the one that masters all the situations, the language of anarchist and voluble intelligence (Ahmed). It was in relation to this poetics of language, always direct but as varied and composed as a landscape, that I finally defined the different theatrical types. And it is in this way that Christian Schiaretti and all the marvelous comedians in Reims have performed them.

As a matter of fact, it was in the course of the rehearsals and performances of *Ahmed le subtil* that we became aware of the fact that our project was much larger than the simple creation of a farce inspired by Molière. For the sight of Ahmed, Rhubarbe, Pompestan, Fenda, Moustache, Camille all coming to life gave us striking evidence of a series of theatrical operations that were still open. And this in turn convinced us of the fact that we could and should dramatize and poeticize the real with the aid of these figures, well beyond the single spectacle whose public reception persuaded us of having achieved our goal.

I remember one evening in the oppressive summer heat of Avignon. Schiaretti and I were having a drink under the plane trees, and as often happens in such vacant moments, we began shooting for the stars. Why not give Ahmed a chance to vent his anger in a monologue directed against the critics who were unable to perceive his literary and theatrical novelty? This was the first idea behind *Ahmed se fâche*. And why not directly address the children who, contrary to the critics, had supported us so vigorously, understanding everything, laughing with everything, even the political allusions to situations from ten years before, which were older than they were (I recall that, composed in 1984, *Ahmed le subtil* was performed in 1994)? And since I was a philosopher, why not let Ahmed – whose capacity for languages knows no limits – address them with a series of philosophy lessons? This was the first intuition of what was to become, one year later, *Ahmed philosophe*. Then, toward this summer's end, I was talking with my friends from the Comédie of Reims about an old project that the death of Vitez had put on hold: a contemporary adaptation of *The Frogs* by Aristophanes, in which the duel between Aeschylus and Euripides would be replaced by a confrontation between Brecht and Claudel, in which Pirandello would play the role of Sophocles, and in which we would find Ahmed who, like the slave Xanthias in Aristophanes, would serve as the guide to Hell not for Dionysus but for Madame Pompestan, promoted for the occasion to Minister of Culture. 'But of course!' said my friends in Reims. And so I undertook the composition of *Les Citrouilles*, the fourth installment of this 'tetralogy' which the publishing house of Actes Sud – who loyally published the text of the plays upon their performance – has had the idea of gathering in a single volume ten years later. For which I am very grateful.

III

Why Ahmed? Why an Algerian? He could certainly have been a black African (as I did not fail to include an African woman, Fenda, among the types of linguistic virtuosity). If I had been German, Ahmed would probably have been Turkish; if I had been Belgian, he would have been Moroccan; if I had been Greek, he would have been Albanian; if I had been Hungarian, he would have been a gypsy; if I had been British, he would have been Pakistani; if I had been a US citizen, he would have been Mexican; and if I had been Italian, it would have sufficed for Ahmed to be Sicilian, Sardinian, Calabrian or even Neapolitan. In all cases, we are dealing with the proletarian who has come 'from the South', the one who has to take care of production and the life of the people from the North, the one whose liberty must at all times be conquered against the resentment and vengefulness of those who live in fear. Whence his endurance, his intelligence, his relentless vitality, and finally his social and linguistic virtuosity. Mao Zedong said: 'The peasants are clear-sighted.'[2] Let us say that the eye of the proletarian from the South sees clearly from afar. This is fortunate for him, because whatever he sees nearby, in his immediate surroundings, is far from shiny: ordinary racism, jealousy of someone whose existence is vast and varied, all kinds of injustice, discriminatory laws, cautiousness, harsh working conditions.... But he sees far, his life is a voyage, his children – whether by ruse, by force or through reason – will have what he never had.

2. *Translator's Note*: An allusion to a famous quotation from Mao Zedong's 'Report on an Investigation of the Peasant Movement in Hunan'. In French, the usual translation of Mao's expression combines the peasantry's sight of what is just (*voit juste*) and what is far (*voit loin*). Badiou will take advantage of this combination so as to play on the difference between what is immediate or close at hand and what is distant or faraway.

And he knows the arcane mysteries of society, precisely because society tries to keep them from him.

On stage this is the true referent of what I call a 'diagonal' character. Since always, he has been a major condition of comedy. The slave animates ancient comedy, just as the servant animates classical comedy. The modern proletarian did not have this function, probably because he was charged with a political mission so that the epic seemed more appropriate for him than the farce. But today this mission is no longer legible, the revolution is no longer an Idea capable of investing the working condition with a sense of seriousness, or even tragedy. So then, set free and at the same time newly subjugated, the proletarian from the South can and must – on the stage and behind the eternal appearance of the mask – bring out the becoming-farcical of the world, traverse and devastate all milieus with his cunning, and turn all the available languages against their natural users. It is this effect that is 'diagonal', in the sense in which the diagonal of the square is incommensurable to its side. In the social square of a world delivered over to capitalist savagery pure and simple, Ahmed complicates the situation to the point where, in and through laughter as well as through its reverse side in doubt and anxiety, another dimension emerges that no longer shares a common measure with this world. In this sense, the fact of his being a 'stranger', someone who has come from elsewhere, serves as a metaphor: in reality, he is from here, but from a 'here' that lies revealed in its imposture and its semblance. Certain spectators have insisted on the 'unreal' nature of Ahmed, as well as on the 'overloaded' dimension of his companions, the Rhubarbs, the Moustaches, the Pompestans.… I take pleasure in these objections. For, as a diagonal character, Ahmed shows that the pure theatrical energy of what is said to be the necessity of the real (the market economy, elections, human rights, Left and Right, the globalization of finance...) can be seen and dismantled as pure discourse. And the figurines of the social game, whom Ahmed does not stop ridiculing and harassing, become on the stage the fragile body and the comic voice of those discourses that Ahmed (who makes better use of them than his professional interlocutors) exhibits as being empty vessels. This frenetic production, in quick theatrical situations, of the void and the obscene pomp of all the available discourses is what makes of Ahmed-the-diagonal-character, in his own way, a philosopher. That is, someone who, by his acts alone, dismantles the stubborn logic of opinions.

IV

People often interrogate me about the relation in my writing between philosophy and farce. How can I move from the enormous conceptual construction of *Being and Event*, loaded with mathematics and the history of thought, to the 'vulgar' turns and the speedy execution of my theatrical scenes? This question is all the more pertinent insofar as, in my conception of comedy, I do not want to give up on the heaviest of puns, nor on triviality, nor on sexual innuendos, nor on the beatings, nor even on the scatological remarks. Moreover, I gladly practice the arbitrary ending, in the genre of the *deus ex machina*, which prohibits me from pretending that the spectacle may deliver a univocal lesson.

Ever since Plato, the relations between philosophy and theatre are both essential and difficult. The philosopher is quick to see in theatre the very example of the dangerous powers of the simulacrum and imitation. The authenticity that he seeks does not easily accommodate the effects of theatricality and its equivocations. Contemporary thought struggles against the allure of representation. Now, what happens, one evening, in the artifice of lights and the borrowed costumes, if not the most glorious form of representation?

A first attempt at a synthesis between philosophy and theatre would be to make the stage into the place for a philosophical didacticism. The situations and characters would certainly be representative, but the referent to be deciphered behind this representation in the end would be a conceptual situation, a typology of forms of consciousness, of which the philosopher furthermore would describe the abstract structure. Sartre's theatre obviously followed along this path, which is not without merits. However, it is not at all sure whether philosophy and theatre emerge unscathed from this operation. Theatre loses therein its poetic energy and philosophy risks being nothing more than a stylization of opinions. Sartre's existentialism, qua philosophy, is probably more homogeneous with this genre of transposition than a project of conceptual (even Platonist) thought such as mine.

My orientation in the end is completely different. I am convinced that theatre in and of itself, through its own resources, constitutes a particularly active form of thought, an act of thought. It is, as Mallarmé used to say, a 'superior' art. And comedy, or the farce, far from being the 'lowly' registers of this thought, are quite on the contrary the purest and most difficult ones, as Hegel saw very well in his aesthetics of the theatre. The farce seeks to capture the circulation of the desire and the immediate intelligence of the situations, to discern the heroism contained within everyday triviality, and to establish, through the delivery of laughter, that any linguistic occurrence whatsoever can become the occasion for the feat of a performance. All this calls for forms that are both new and tested, consistent and volatile, as is shown in an exemplary fashion in cinema, in the work of Charlie Chaplin.

When I write theatre, I do not start from philosophy. I start from the theatre and this is all the more true in the case of the last three plays in the tetralogy, written for the actors, lighting engineers, musicians, costume and set designers, technicians, and director of the Comédie in Reims. I attend the improvisations, the rehearsals, and it is the physics of the scene on stage that feeds the chemistry of the words.

Why, then, *Ahmed philosophe*? In thirty-two sketches, philosophy is not present there where it declares it is, that is, in Ahmed's speeches. It would not be too difficult (though quite useless) to show that his aim is to overpower his interlocutor, to lead him astray with his language, to emphasize and show off a dimension of his sovereignty that is at once theatrical and subjective. We could also study how the 'arguments' that would seem to be philosophical more often than not are pure sophistries whose inconsistency is hidden from view only thanks to Ahmed's theatrical virtuosity (his quick feet, his adaptation to his interlocutors, or his violent desire to seduce the public). The situations, which are like snapshots, command the appearance of an inventive language, one that circulates between the concepts and the concrete annotations for the sole purpose of 'proving' that the freedom of the spirit is a form of happiness and the linguistic force of thought is a form of joy. When Ahmed showers Moustache with woolly considerations on the inside and the outside, the point is ultimately to keep him from taking a leak, which is the only thing that Moustache really feels the urge to do. When Fenda multiplies the objections to Ahmed's considerations about the notion of time, it is in order to convince him that, after all, they could love each other without delay. When, before Rhubarb, Ahmed launches into abstract reflections on the topic of measures, on the relativity of large and small, it is only to take literally the expression 'péter plus haut que son cul' ('to fart higher than one's ass')[3] and to demonstrate, once more, the mediocrity of Rhubarbe's 'democratic' consciousness. When Madame Pompestan tries hard to define for Ahmed the notions of 'law' and 'French nationality', it is only to give Ahmed another occasion for the violent affirmation – if necessary with the use of his stick – that the only rule worth following is to leave in peace the people who live here, wherever they come from. And even when Ahmed's monologue is about the infinite or the multiple, it is in order to allow the extreme theatrical concentration, with the body seized by the vertigo of words bouncing off from the public, to soothe the masked hero's anxiety and anonymous solitude.

In *Ahmed philosophe*, the explicit philosophy is cheap rubbish. It is the raw material for the play, that of Ahmed as much as of the other protagonists. It is just a linguistic register, one among others, which is available to the diagonal character. Even the concepts, which give the sketches their title (the nothing, the infinite, the nation, chance, death, the multiple, the subject, and so on), serve to designate a theatrical situation that is most often sampled from fixed expressions in ordinary language. Take the sketch titled 'Chance'. The basic schema for it comes directly from the burlesque tradition: a flowerpot repeatedly falls on Moustache's head. In order to convince Moustache to come back to the place where the flowerpot will drop, Ahmed is going to wax rhetorical about chance, involving his victim in the experiment of a farcical lesson about the distinction between chance and necessity. Sure, Ahmed knows – and transposes into his own language which is both abstract and rich in images – the theory of chance formulated in the nineteenth

3. *Translator's Note*: The French colloquial expression *péter plus haut que son cul* is the equivalent of the equally vulgar and colloquial 'to think one is hot shit'.

century by the French philosopher Cournot: chance is the encounter of two independent causal series (in our case, Moustache's walking and the flowerpot's falling).[4] But evidently this is all just a trick; and the 'theory' serves only to hypnotize Moustache. Schiaretti came up with the brilliant idea – a true theatre-idea – of showing the trick for everyone to see: Ahmed is actually holding a cord in his hand that is attached to the flowerpot by way of a pulley. When he makes pompous predictions about chance, he gives one end of the cord to Moustache, who holds on to it without paying much attention, and without understanding the trick – all concentrated as he is, with the good will of stupidity, on Ahmed's explanations. All this makes it immediately palpable that the philosophical discourse offers raw materials for theatre, as a language captured by the intrigues and artifices of the farce.

Nevertheless, this kind of scene touches upon philosophy in two different ways. First, because, in passing, the philosophical discourse caught up in the dynamics of the theatre also makes itself understood after all, and, thus, we can enjoy its virtuosity, its variety, its victory. Second, and above all, because each situation on the stage shows us that to think the situation, and to do so quickly and in a language of one's control, is a boundless source of gaiety and power, even and especially when one finds oneself in a sinister and oppressive social environment. The 'proletarian from the South', whether it is in relation to the notables and enemies, in the societal game, in the persecution to which he falls prey, or in the complications of sexual intrigue, can draw reassurance

4. *Translator's Note*: Antoine Augustin Cournot (1801–1877) was a French mathematician, economist, and philosopher. He began to formulate his theory of chance as the encounter of two independent causal chains in works such as his 1851 *Essai sur les fondements de nos connaissances et sur les caractères de la critique philosophique*.

and clairvoyance from the act of thinking and speaking. Yes, this is philosophy – as *gai savoir*, as gay or joyous science.

V

This joyous science explains why I wrote *Ahmed philosophe* for the children. What does 'for the children' mean? I certainly do not believe that we need a theatre especially reserved for children. On the contrary, I would gladly assert that children are the most demanding and the most lucid part of the public. They are the ones who desire the most that we respect them and address them without condescension and without demagoguery. Every childhood, like my own, by nature stands in a deep relation to the theatre, for every childhood knows the nature of play, its importance and its truth. If I wrote *Ahmed philosophe* for the children it is because I believed that the joyous science of this genre of 'philosophy' could find an appropriate expression only in an elementary theatre (in the sense of the elements air, fire, and earth): a pure theatre. What should we understand by this? Theatre today is most often heavy-handed. It is materially heavy (productions that conspicuously show off the money invested in them, through opera-style decor, and so on) and it is spiritually heavy (filled with morose sentiments, complaints, sad nihilism, compassion…). This heavy-handedness in my view is the result of a general resignation of sorts, which by contrast is completely external to the resourcefulness and force of thought that I wish to typify on the stage. Whence the need for a form of theatre that is certainly 'perfect' (virtuosity of the actors, infinite care given to the lighting, simple beauty of the arrangement of the stage setting, belaboured language both rude and poetic) but also light and pure, that is to say, a form of theatre that is essential, frontal, energetic and that demands the support of the public in the form of laughter, presence of mind, and concentration. A theatre whose purity and mobility shakes up the fearful gloom and doom of established opinions. I would like for the theatre not to be a mirror, or a redoubling, of the confused, frenetic and stagnant world to which the sombre dictatorship of profit confines us. I would like it to be a lightning strike, an elucidation, and an exhortation.

Of such a theatre, children can be the guarantors and the judges. They will thus be charged with the task of swaying the other parts of the public, of making them accept the subtleties of laughter and the distance with regard to themselves.

This willful search for a 'pure' theatre has governed the choice of the forms that I adopted in *Ahmed philosophe*: short scenes that oblige one to concentrate the totality of a theatrical situation in a few pages; never more than two characters – which leads us back to the true source of theatricality: either the soliloquy or else the conflict; the systematic use of the archetypes of the farce: the deceptions, the disguise, the beatings, the pursuits, the biological functions (pissing, farting, screwing, picking one's nose...), parody; a language that is both tight and poetic, welcoming puns, approximations, insults but also images, evocations, as well as concepts, nonsense, 'proofs' in the genre of Molière's (Sganarelle trying to prove the existence of God to Don Juan);[5] improvisations both verbal and gestural; and a rapid and colourful kind of limpidity, which puts into play a secondary solemnity, tied to the fact that nothing is

5. *Translator's Note*: Sganarelle appears in several of Molière's plays, most famously in *Sganarelle, or, the Self-Deceived Husband* and *The Doctor in Spite of Himself*. Badiou here is referring to a scene from Molière's *Don Juan*.

forbidden, nothing is set in advance, so that the point of the real of this world is conveyed through the fiction of its interstices, through its secret shadows, when everything, precisely, is shown in full daylight.

Such a theatre – wholly and entirely shown, material, and explicit – is a wager for thought over and against death. 'Down with death!' says Ahmed. I now would like to express the extent to which those artists in France or Italy who have tackled this text head-on have been faithful to this maxim. *Ahmed philosophe* is a very demanding spectacle. Because of the brevity of the sketches, the actors have no time to catch up; from the first moment on, they must be perfect in their performance. Because of the energy demanded by the typical practices of the farce, they must keep their body and voice extremely disciplined. Because of the variety of the situations, which follow one another in quick succession, the director, the lighting engineers and the musicians must invent a rhythmic scansion of the utmost precision. The slightest slip-up, the shortest waste of time, are immediately visible during the play. A pure theatre is also a particularly exposed theatre. 'Down with death!' also means: the theatre, during every second of such a spectacle, must produce and support its life. No lateral artifice, no heavy symbolism, no spectacular effect, no endless reflection can come and relieve the theatre of this duty. Whatever I wrote does not protect the artists on the stage but rather commits them and wears them down. In *Ahmed se fâche*, Camille at one point complains that thinking is tiresome. The Ahmed cycle invites the spectators to the joy of such a tiresome experience of excellence.

VI

The tetralogy inflects the active relation of thinking to the theatre in four very different forms. I have already indicated the violent singularity of the very short sketches in *Ahmed philosophe. Ahmed le subtil* is a comedy of intrigues, with all the usual suspects of the genre: the young against the old, the oppressed against the notables; the disguises, the lies, the quid pro quos and the recognition scenes; the reversals of fortune and the violent turns. *Ahmed se fâche* is already a more meditative and nocturnal play. It is an odd ragbag: slightly surrealist (there is Spiderman, Athena, a parody of Romeo and Juliet, the lyrical monologue of the firefighters, Ahmed's double), with themes from actuality that are still provocative today (what is an Arab?), and a vein of melancholy around the couple of Ahmed and Camille. It is a play with no subject other than the dispersed poetry of the figures assembled therein. *Les Citrouilles* is the most ambitious and the most developed construction in the cycle. In any case it is the one that I prefer, if an author may have the right to say which one of his own works he prefers. Situated in Hell, the play offers a kind of assessment of the state of theatre in the twentieth century. In it, we meet Brecht, Claudel or Pirandello, not only as characters but also in more or less deformed quotations that are everywhere stuffed into the text itself. Ultimately, what is at stake is to tell the public that theatre can exist with the same powerfulness as when Aristophanes put the great tragic playwrights on the stage. The chorus – indeed there is a chorus, composed of giants from the mountain – says as much and I can conclude with these words:

Thus the stage shows us that in everyone the path of the decision,
The changing of directions of existence,
Happens by tearing one away from the mechanisms of the self,
And by secretly consenting
To what runs counter to our comfort.[6]

6. *Translator's Note*: These lines appear toward the end of *Les Citrouilles* and, as a lesson in the depths of self-sacrifice, they are meant to sway the public in favour of choosing Claudel over Brecht as *the* playwright of the twentieth century, only to be followed in the next scene by an equal amount of support for Brecht. 'Let us declare them to be equals, under the universal eye of the theatre', concludes Ahmed. See Alain Badiou, *La Tétralogie d'Ahmed: Ahmed le subtil, Ahmed philosophe, Ahmed se fâche, Les Citrouilles* (Arles: Actes Sud, 2009), 524–5.

6

THREE QUESTIONS TO THE AUTHOR

You have written two pieces, Ahmed le subtil *and now* Les Citrouilles, *by tracing the model of famous comedies from Antiquity. Why?*

My first response will be extremely simple. I have always been struck by the extraordinary liberty with which our great playwrights rewrote the Greek tragedies or stole a Spanish comedy, sometimes almost literally, and by how all this, in spite of the evident borrowings, produced works that were absolutely singular and unique. Very early on I had the idea that in theatre, here I am talking really of theatre as art, the theatrical and artistic force is not necessarily, nor even primarily, linked to the original invention of the plot, setting, or situation. I would gladly defend the thesis that in reality there are a limited number of theatrical resources, like a stock repertoire, which is constituted early on and from which everyone can draw freely. From this repertoire, one naturally picks the most finished forms, those that have already refined the raw materials, and on their basis one invents. But one invents on the basis of an existing code or framework, both of which have given proof of their efficacy. This is the first element. More profoundly, I think that this question is also related to the idea that I form for myself about the current situation of theatre and its relation to its own history. We all know the view of contemporary theatre according to which it would find itself in a unique, pathetic and slightly deadly situation. This is the idea that theatre would have great difficulty even to exist, that its very being stands on shaky grounds, which brings with it the notion that theatre is now completely cut off from its tradition. It is strange to note that in the life of the theatre today we find two facts side by side, in a rather paradoxical way: the constant emphasis placed on restaging the great classical plays and on devoting new, sumptuous or innovative productions to them; and a contemporary creative scene in which the general conviction holds that it is nearly impossible to write a theatre text – to the point where people either resort to non-theatrical materials or else consider that the general rules for theatrical writing have become obsolete. I am struck by this coincidence, which we likewise find in other arts as well, between a tendency to reduce everything to the museum, to the guided visits of the great treasures from the past, on the one hand, and, on the other, a contemporary creation that would cultivate a certain aspect of exhaustion, of impasse, of the end of the world. This simply is not my view of things. In any case, even if it were true, it would make me rather sad, and I would prefer to think that it is not like that! I care for the notion that theatre constructs its own modernity in relation to its past and that this relation is affirmative in nature. I am convinced that theatre today is capable of taking up the challenge of its own past. For this reason, you will understand that one of the technical tricks, for me, is to measure oneself (myself) up against the great plays from the past to see what kind of contemporary inscription can be accomplished based on them. I would like to clarify that I do not see this as a universal method. I do not consider this to be an obligation for all, far from it. But nevertheless can this challenge be taken up? From what I often hear, it does not seem to be self-evident to return to the plays from Antiquity. And yet this is precisely what interests me: to know if this is possible. Finally, the last reason is that of the comical, of the contemporary comedy, which is very close to my heart. Is it possible to produce a contemporary comedy without abandoning that great vocation of the comical which is to produce types, to try and inscribe on the stage something which functions in the way of the typical figures of our contemporary world? To this I should add that for Aristophanes the true subject-matter of the play is a topic of literary aesthetics, through the extremely detailed debate between Aeschylus and Euripides. I have imitated this by constructing a picaresque episode for the descent into Hell, and, for the real centre of gravity of the play, that is, the discussion of theatrical aesthetics, it is obviously no longer Aeschylus and Euripides but Claudel and Brecht whom I have called upon.

You are a philosopher and a playwright. Does one of these two dominate the other?

As far as I'm concerned, I have no idea of any hierarchy in the varied exercise – as varied as possible – of my faculties. Kant used to say that ultimately the ideal or the duty of each one was to give the largest possible playing field to the multiplicity of one's faculties. This principle suits me rather well. So there is philosophy and there is theatre, I certainly cannot completely prohibit a certain circulation between the two, whether visible or invisible to my own eyes, but a hierarchy? I think not! Theatre presents for me an extraordinary space of freedom. Philosophy, after all, is in a certain sense also my profession, which accordingly generates a series of very complex and burdensome conditions. It is also caught in the constraints of a form of thought that seeks out rigour and consistency in its construction. Finally, as we know, philosophy is also from its very origin a bit unsure of its own status. It raises the question of what it is and goes to great lengths to answer this question. This is not the case of theatre. When I feel like writing a theatre play, or when, as has been the case since the wonderful collaboration with the Comédie of Reims, I am commissioned to produce a play, this for me is a magnificent space for freedom. And, contrary to what one might think, the commission only augments this space, no doubt because in that case one writes frontally or directly: someone speaks, that is how it begins, someone is there, says something, and you see what happens afterward! This is a great joy. You play it by ear. The novelist can write in isolation, or by addressing only himself, but in theatre this is not possible. There always is a moment when one asks oneself: If I were the spectator what would I understand by what I am writing? So this is a very different practice, one that is really very different from philosophical writing. As a result, when I write for the theatre, I have the impression of being at a far remove from the philosopher that I am. Of course, this goes even further from the moment I discuss during the rehearsals with the people from the theatre company. I see how the whole thing is being transformed, in ways that moreover are always a bit bizarre, because it never turns out to be what one had imagined. On the other hand, for me this would create a shared destiny between these two forms of writing and would bring the two together, whereas they have been opposed, or almost, for a very long time – with Plato already condemning and opposing the theatre. This goes back to what I invoked in answer to the first question, namely, the fact that in philosophy, too, or above all, the dominant theme is that of the end. A large part of contemporary thought is entirely governed by the idea that philosophy is over and done with and that we are in the period of the end of metaphysics, that the ensemble of the ideals of modern rationalism are entirely inoperative, and so on. This is an atmosphere that resembles a kind of organized twilight. Since this idea exists as well for the theatre, I could say, using a military metaphor, that on this front I am engaged in a parallel combat. And theatre, especially comedy, is then the active, public and joyous figure of a polemic against the idea of the end.

Four of your plays have been produced at the Comédie of Reims. Has this adventure changed anything in your way of writing or in your view of the theatre?

Undoubtedly. I wrote *Ahmed le subtil* in isolation, for my own pleasure, and the play was left lying dormant for a long time. By contrast, the creation of what is now a tetralogy, with Ahmed as its Wotan, took place in increasingly close collaboration with the group of people from the Comédie of Reims as a whole. Its director, of course, but also its entire troupe, its set designer, its costume designer, its facilities – all this has brought the writing closer to the materiality of the theatre. There is, after all, something very strange in the kind of disorderly and at the same time attentive collective, both passionate and susceptible, of the theatre world. Of course, I began to write already knowing more or less that it would be such or such an actor who was certain or most likely to play this or that role, that Didier Galas with his mask would play Ahmed, and so on. All this is incorporated into the writing. I would like to defend the idea that, here too, when you are able to think in greater proximity to the theatre, the freedom of writing augments and does not diminish. This allows one to draw from the theatre itself certain ideas that the writing on its own finally would not have produced. In this regard I would like to insist that the work with the Comédie of Reims and the regime of being commissioned to write have increased what I always felt in the writing of theatre: a sense of freedom. A freedom which is not simply a fantasy or a dream and which I like to call a material freedom. One is more aware of what the theatre is capable of when one writes at its service and within its structure. It is there, finally, that I have learned that the theatre is always capable of more than one thinks and that, in reality, when one writes far away from the theatre, one is intimidated by it as though its possibilities were limited. When you come closer, you realize on the contrary that its resources are immense, infinite even.

SOURCES

CHAPTER 1

'Rhapsody for the Theatre: A Short Philosophical Treatise' is the translation of Alain Badiou, *Rhapsodie pour le théâtre: Court traité philosophique* (Paris: L'Imprimerie Nationale, 1990). Currently out of print, the French version of this book is part of a series called 'Le Spectateur français'. An earlier English translation appeared in *Theatre Survey* 49.2 (November 2008), pp. 187–238. For their editorial assistance during the preparation of this earlier version, the translator wishes to thank Martin Puchner and David Kornhaber.

CHAPTER 2

'Theatre and Philosophy' is the translation of *Théâtre et philosophie*, a talk presented during a meeting in May 1998 in the bar of the Comédie of Reims and issued by Noria as a small brochure or notebook (Cahier

13). Subsequently, the text also appears in *Frictions* 2 (Spring–Summer 2000), pp. 133–41.

CHAPTER 3

'The Political Destiny of Theatre Yesterday and Today' is the translation of Badiou's preface, 'Destin politique du théâtre, hier, maintenant', in Jonny Ebstein, Philippe Ivernel, Monique Surel-Tupin and Sylvie Thomas, eds., *Au temps de l'anarchie, un théâtre de combat, 1880–1914* (Paris: Séguier-Archimbaud, 2001), vol. 1, pp. 7–14.

CHAPTER 4

'Notes on Jean-Paul Sartre's *The Condemned of Altona*' is the translation of 'Notes sur *Les Séquestrés d'Altona*', *Revue internationale de philosophie* 231 (2005), pp. 51–60.

CHAPTER 5

'The Ahmed Tetralogy' is part of an unpublished typescript, *Le Cycle Ahmed: Un projet de théâtre contemporain*, collectively signed by La Comédie de Reims, with synopses of the four plays, and texts by the director Christian Schiaretti and the playwright Badiou. Originally titled 'Ahmed: la diagonale du carré de la scène' ('Ahmed: The Diagonal of the Square of the Stage'), this part of *Le Cycle Ahmed* also appears as the preface to the set of Badiou's Ahmed plays published in a single volume, *La Tétralogie d'Ahmed* (Arles: Actes Sud, 2009), pp. 9–28.

CHAPTER 6

'Three Questions to the Author', previously unpublished, also appears in the typescript *Le Cycle Ahmed*, pp. 22–5.

INDEX